The Psalms in Daily Life

JOHN ROGERSON

Published in Great Britain in 2001 by
Society for Promoting Christian Knowledge
Holy Trinity Church
Marylebone Road
London NW1 4DU

British Library Cataloguing-in-Publication Data

A catalogue record for this book is available from the British Library

ISBN 0-281 05141 0

Typeset by David Gregson Associates
Printed in Great Britain by
The Cromwell Press, Trowbridge

Contents

Introduction

Several years ago I published some daily Bible study notes on se-
lected psalms for the Bible Reading Fellowship series 'Guidelines'.
I deliberately chose psalms that were less well known, as well as
psalms that lamented the apparent absence or inaction of God in
the face of the psalmists' troubles. I tried to relate these psalms
to the situations of believers living in today's world. Such was
the generous response of users of these notes that it became apparent that there was a need for a small book on the Psalms that
took this approach further. I am grateful to SPCK for agreeing
to publish such a book, and for waiting longer than had been envisaged for its completion. Even a retired professor can be so
busy that projects get delayed!

The translation of the Psalms is my own, from the Hebrew text
as it has come down to us. As anyone who has translated the
Psalms will know, they present many difficulties, and no translator
or translation panel will ever produce a version with which
every expert will agree! In my own case I have been bolder than
might be possible for a panel of translators, and I have erred on
the side of trying to bring out the force of the Hebrew, perhaps
at the cost of its poetry. I have made no attempt to produce a
translation in inclusive language. While I always write in inclusive
language, I believe that translations should indicate the gender
weighting of the source text. This is also the view taken by a
number of feminists.

The experience of engaging closely with the Hebrew text has
reinforced my conviction that the Psalms are too important

simply to be used selectively in worship. As the writer of Psalm 1 insists, they must be studied deeply. They come from situations that, in their way, were as problematic and puzzling for people with faith in God as are the situations which face believers in today's world. The psalmists' world, like ours, was one in which powerful interests rode roughshod over the poor and over the demands of justice; it was a world in which power corrupted those who held it, in which anyone who stood up for what was right was regarded as a nuisance. It was a world in which religion could be used as a cloak for power and injustice. It was also a world from which God often seemed to be absent, or one in which he seemed powerless, if present. In the face of these difficulties, the psalmists held on to their conviction that God would have the last word, and that their hopes for a world from which had been banished war, injustice, poverty, dishonesty and cruelty, including cruelty to nature, were not the insanities of incurable dreamers. They dared to view things from the perspective of God's completed work, and to believe that processes were in operation that were leading to that completion. They thus lived and believed dialectically, that is, they lived in an ambiguous world to which they added a vision that gave it coherence and meaning. This vision came neither from the world itself nor from their own resources, but from received traditions which they had embraced as a result of teaching, worship and the testing of their own experience.

It must never be forgotten that the Psalms are Jewish texts. From New Testament times, however, they were taken over by the Christian Church and used in many ways. They were associated, as in Judaism, with the life of David; they were seen as prophecies of Christ's death and resurrection, and the spread of the gospel. They became a fundamental part of Christian worship. The interpretations of the Psalms in the present work are the work of a Christian, but they recognize their Jewish origins by being understood as the expressions of ordinary faithful Jewish people who were trying to make sense of an ambiguous and in some ways cruel world in terms of a hope for a better world that only God could bring. Their utterances, because they were often the cries of bewildered, pressurized folk, contain sentiments that are vindictive and self-centred; but that is part of their value as utterances of real, honest people. The psalmists say the kind of things that we say, or might say, faced with similar difficulties; but they also rise above these natural human frailties and express hopes that are truly God-given, and valid for all times and all places.

The most difficult decision in writing the book has been how to put the psalms that are treated into chapters. This is because it is never easy to pigeon-hole psalms, such is their variety and richness of content. The solution adopted is inevitably a compromise. The first two chapters, 'Psalms of Personal Distress' and 'Psalms Crying Out for Justice', represent my own classification based upon content. The chapter entitled 'The Penitential Psalms' deals with the seven psalms of that name in Christian tradition, psalms associated with Lent and Passiontide, although I have tried to avoid an explicitly Christian interpretation of them. Chapters 4 and 6, entitled 'Psalms of Zion' and 'Royal Psalms', use classifications suggested by modern scholarship, based on theories of the origin of these psalms, theories which I have mostly ignored. Only some of what modern scholars have designated as Royal Psalms are dealt with here. Finally, the title of chapter 5, 'Psalms of Ascents' uses a title found in the Hebrew Bible, while 'Other Psalms' of chapter 7 needs no comment. Because psalms cannot easily be pigeon-holed several psalms could just as well go into different chapters from those in which they actually appear; the arrangement is a compromise. It is to be hoped, however, that the chapters will make the book more user-friendly, and will be seen to be more than purely arbitrary.

I

Psalms of Personal Distress

Psalm 4

1   When I call, answer me, God who defends my cause;
    when I was under pressure you gave me space:
    be gracious to me and hear my prayer.
2   You who see only human things:
    how long will you insult the God I glorify?
    You love what is empty and you seek what is false.
3   Know that the Lord has done marvellous things* for his
        faithful one.
    The Lord hears when I call to him.
4   Tremble and do not sin.
    Ponder in the privacy of your heart and on your couch,
    and silence your slanders.
5   Offer the appointed sacrifices, and trust in the Lord.
6   Many say, 'Oh that we might see some good!
    The favour of the Lord has gone from us.'
7   You, God, put more joy in my heart
    than when their corn and wine are abundant.
8   In peace will I lie down and sleep;
    you alone enable me to live in safety.

* Reading, with many Hebrew manuscripts, *hiphla'* for the traditional *hiphlah*

The closing words of this psalm are most likely to claim our attention, and they account for the fact that it has traditionally been

used in services at the end of the day. Peaceful sleep is something that is becoming increasingly difficult for many people in a world in which noise and stress are on the increase. The psalmist also seems to have had good reasons for wanting peaceful sleep, given the difficult time that he was having with his opponents.

Some details of the psalm are difficult. In verse 2, for example, the traditional translation 'how long will you dishonour my glory' implies that the speaker is God, for who else could otherwise talk about 'my glory'? The ancient Greek and Latin translations of this verse, evidently following a slightly different Hebrew text, have 'how long will you be heavy of heart?', which can be found in several modern Roman Catholic translations. The translation given above implies that the speaker is the psalmist, and that he is addressing his opponents, who do not honour God. Another difficulty is at verse 6, where many translations have 'Lord, lift up the light of your countenance upon us.'

In spite of several uncertainties, we can see two parties in this psalm: those who doubt whether there is any point in doing good or in seeking God, and the psalmist whose confidence in God enables him to sleep soundly and safely. The former are told to stop scheming and devising evil plans (verse 4) and to worship God appropriately (verse 5). The psalmist is able to see things from a broad perspective (verse 1b), and this is the basis of his hope especially if, taking verses 6 and 7 together, the psalmist's opponents have experienced bad harvests.

To see things from a narrow perspective, one in which trivial matters assume giant proportions, is to be in a situation in which sleep may become difficult and action may be hindered. To see things from a broad perspective, best of all, the perspective of eternity, means that things are put in proportion, and begin to lose their power to disturb and control us. This does not mean that we simply accommodate ourselves to evil by an adjustment of the mind. After all, the psalmist is not exactly passive in his attitude to his opponents! It means that we let God's gift of seeing reality in terms of eternity control all that we do, whether it is praying, arguing or sleeping.

Psalm 22

1 My God, my God, why have you forsaken me?
The words of my groaning bring me no deliverance.

2 My God, I have cried to you by day and got no answer,
and by night and gained no respite.

3 Yet you are the Holy One,
enthroned upon the praises of Israel.

4 It was in you that our fathers trusted –
trusted, and you delivered them.

5 It was to you that they cried and you delivered them;
it was you that they trusted and were not put to shame.

6 As for me, I am a worm, not a man,
a scorn of men and despised by the people.

7 All who see me laugh scornfully at me;
they gape at me and shake their heads:

8 'Let him lean on the Lord – he will deliver him!
He will rescue him, for he is his favourite!'

9 But you did help me burst from the womb,
and did lay me upon my mother's breasts.

10 I have depended on you since my birth,
and you have been my God even from my mother's womb.

11 Do not desert me, for trouble is at hand
and there is no one else to help.

12 I am surrounded by many wild oxen;
strong bulls of Bashan encircle me.

13 They come at me with open mouths
like lions that tear their prey and roar.

14 I am like water poured on the ground,
and all my bones are out of joint.
My heart is like wax
melting into my bowels.

15 My mouth is dry like a piece of clay pot,
and my tongue is glued fast to my gums.
You are laying me in the dust of death.

16 For dogs have come at me from all sides,
    a band of wrong-doers has surrounded me;
    my hands and my feet are like a lion's.
17 I can count all my bones;
    my enemies look up and stare at me.
18 They parcel out my garments among them
    and cast lots for my clothes.
19 As for you, Lord, do not be absent;
    you, my helper, come to my aid!
20 Save me from the sword,
    my life from the power of the dogs.
21 Deliver me from the mouth of the lion,
    and from the horns of the wild oxen.

    You have answered me!
22 I will tell stories of your renown to my brothers;
    I will praise you within the congregation.
23 Praise the Lord, all you who fear him,
    honour him, all you seed of Jacob,
    be in awe of him, all you seed of Israel!
24 For he has not abhorred or despised
    the affliction of the poor;
    he has not hidden his face from him,
    but has heard when he cried to him.
25 Because of you I can praise you in the great congregation;
    I shall perform my vows in the presence of all who fear you.
26 The poor will eat and be satisfied;
    those who seek the Lord will praise him.
    May their hearts live for ever!
27 All the ends of the earth will remember
    and will return to the Lord,
    and all the families of the nations
    will fall down in worship before him.
28 For kingship belongs to the Lord,
    and he rules over the nations.
29 The fat ones of the world will also fall down in worship to him;

those who go down to the grave will kneel before him
and will not save their own lives.
30 Posterity will serve him;
stories will be told of the Lord to future generations.
31 They shall come and recount his saving deeds
to a people not yet born,
that he, the Lord, has done it.

The fact that this psalm changes abruptly from lament to praise at
verse 22 has not only given rise to the suggestion that two originally independent psalms have been joined together; it gives rise
to several theories about how the psalm is to be understood.
One suggestion is that it was recited when a sufferer who had
been delivered came to the temple to give thanks for his deliverance. The emphasis then falls upon the thanksgiving part of the
psalm, but entails that the troubles described in the first part are
all in the past. If this is correct, it would be necessary to translate
the opening words as 'My God, my God, why did you forsake
me?' and this is certainly possible. Another suggestion is that
while the speaker was pouring out his heart to God in his complaint, a priest or temple official delivered a message of hope to
him, assuring him that all would be well. As a result, he moved
instantly from lament to praise. The view taken here is that the
psalmist's complaint is an actual one and that, as he prays, a
sudden insight of faith enables him to picture his deliverance as
accomplished.

The opening words are the most poignant expression anywhere
in the Psalter of the anguish of being deserted by God. The
word translated 'groaning' in verse 1 has the sense of 'roaring',
while the verbs rendered 'cried' and 'got no answer' imply that
it is fervent and repeated entreaty that go consistently unheard.
The psalmist perceives a contradiction between God's silence,
and the nation's stories about how God had delivered the people
when they prayed to him. Although he only hints at his troubles,
they seem to include the signs and symptoms of a grave illness,
things that are quickly seized upon by his neighbours as

indications of God's punishment. They mock him savagely, and cynically invite him to trust in God.

The psalmist recalls all the reasons why he *should* commit himself. He is aware that, from birth, God was, as it were, the midwife that enabled him to burst from the womb (verse 9a), and he remembers many divine mercies ever since. However, the troubles that press upon him assume grotesque and terrifying forms as he likens them to bulls of Bashan (verse 12; Bashan, the present-day Golan heights, was and still is famed for its cattle, and the image will not be lost on anyone who has been surrounded or chased by cows or a bull). These troubles threaten his very life, and the images of verses 14–15 can be compared to passages in the Old Testament that describe the ending of life (compare 2 Samuel 14.14 'we must all die, we are like water spilt on the ground'; Ezekiel 37.1–2, the valley of dry bones; Genesis 3.19 'to dust you shall return'). The actions of those around him reinforce the imminence of death as they divide up his property as though he were already dead (verses 16–18). The familiar translation 'they pierce my hands and my feet' represents the traditional link between this psalm and the passion of Jesus, and goes back to the ancient Greek, Latin and Syriac translations of the psalms. The Hebrew has 'my hands and my feet [are] like a lion', which could refer to their grotesquely large appearance in relation to the rest of his emaciated body (as we can see in pictures of starved prisoners of war or of concentration camp victims). Renewed prayer to God leads to the exclamation of faith – 'You have answered me!' (verse 21).

The section that follows is not merely a personal thanksgiving, but is directed towards the whole congregation. The psalmist is not an isolated individual, and his faith is not a private affair. His hope of deliverance is grounded in God's universal kingship and the fact that God has a special concern for the poor and needy. The final note of hope is expressed in verse 30 by reference to those yet unborn, who will be able to hear of and experience God's salvation.

It will always be difficult to read and use this psalm without thinking of Jesus's quotation of its opening words on the cross (Matthew 27.46; Mark 15.34); and we can only imperfectly guess at what the feeling of desertion by God might mean for someone for whom, unlike us, the reality of God's presence was the ground of his being. On most, if not all, of the occasions when we use this psalm we shall not be at death's door, and when we reach that state we shall probably not feel well enough to derive much benefit from it. What we can do is to try to be infected by the psalmist's faith. At death's door he was suddenly able to look beyond his immediate troubles to the majesty of God and to the hope that his kingdom is the ultimate and true reality. This was not the desperate hope of human helplessness projecting its needs on to an imaginary supernatural being. It was the cry of someone who could pray, not in a general way to any God, but to *my* God, who was sustained by the memory of past mercies and nourished by the traditions of a community of faith; the cry of someone who had experienced God's faithfulness and who had come to the inner assurance that that faithfulness would never prove to be an illusion. Perhaps this way of reading the psalm will also bring us close to what it may have meant to Jesus on the cross.

Psalm 38

1   Lord, do not condemn me in your anger,
      nor punish me in your wrath.

2   For your arrows have rained down upon me,
      and your hand has pressed hard upon me.

3   Because of your indignation no part of my body is unscathed;
      because of my sin, no bone is healthy.

4   Like a flood have my wrong-doings gone over my head,
      like a burden too heavy for me to bear.

5   Because of my folly my wounds stink and fester.

6   My body is bent so low,
that I go like a mourner all day long.

7   My loins are filled with the burning of fever,
and no part of my body is spared.

8   I am completely numb and battered,
my inner groaning becomes a roar.

9   My desire, Lord, is known to you,
and my sighing is not hidden from you.

10   My heart beats heavily, I have no strength,
my eyes are dull.

11   My friends and companions avoid me in my sickness
and my relatives stay away,

12   while those who wish me dead strike at me,
and those who mean to injure me spread gossip,
and mutter slander the whole day long.

13   But I am like a deaf man who hears nothing,
and like a dumb man who does not open his mouth.

14   Thus I have become a man who does not hear
and whose mouth utters no defence.

15   For you, Lord, are my hope,
and you will answer, O Lord my God.

16   For I said, 'Do not let them rejoice over me,
those who exult when my foot slips.'

17   I am on the point of stumbling
and my pain is constantly with me.

18   But I confess my wrong-doing
and I am troubled by my sin.

19   Those who are needlessly my enemies are many,
as are those who hate me wrongly.

20   Those who reward good with evil
are against me because I seek what is good.

21   Do not abandon me, Lord;
do not keep away from me, O my God.

22   Make speed to help me,
O Lord, my salvation.

It is hard enough to face serious illness and death while surrounded by the prayers and loving support of family, friends and medical staff. To have to face serious illness and death while coping with the deliberate absence of family and friends plus the active hostility of opponents who have no grounds for their enmity, must be a superhuman task. No reason is given in the psalm for the evasive action taken by the psalmist's family and friends, but it may be that he was suffering from a contagious fever (verse 7) or an illness whose bodily ravages were such that those closest to the psalmist could not bear to look at him (verse 5). But there may have been a deeper reason for the reaction of the friends and foes – the deep-seated belief in the ancient world that bodily perfection and good health were signs of divine favour (compare 1 Samuel 16.12) and that deformity and illness were signs of divine displeasure. If the psalmist had spent a lifetime trying to do what was good (verse 20) and trying faithfully to serve God, then his plight would give satisfaction to anyone who had found his stance uncomfortable or inconvenient. It would be the necessary proof that the psalmist had been mistaken in his commitment to what was good, and would be evidence for a morally grey and indifferent world. Rumours about the psalmist's real or secret life, as opposed to his public life, would spread like wildfire, and offer a cynical explanation for the psalmist's distress.

That the psalmist also believed that his trouble came from God is indicated by the opening verses. But he was also ready to acknowledge his wrong-doings and his frailties (verses 17–18) and he did not surrender his conviction that he had indeed tried to do what was good, and that his opponents were in the wrong. In the last analysis, the psalmist's belief in the goodness of God (verses 15, 21) is more enduring than the common theories that mechanically link human prosperity with divine favour.

Today, the cultivation of health, fitness and perfect looks has been commercialized on a vast scale and religion, in the various guises of healing therapies and wholeness philosophies, has become a partner in the enterprise. It is a natural human response to coping with life, but one that is shallow and which leaves many questions unanswered. Psalm 38 pulls no punches and sweeps nothing under the carpet. It realistically acknowledges that human life is limited, and that a feature of it may be pain, abandonment and hostility that brook no answer. Does God help or provide an answer in such circumstances? The fact that the psalmist dared to believe so when so much seemed to count against such belief, should inspire us to do the same.

Psalm 39

1   I said, 'I will watch what I say
so that I do not sin with my tongue.
I will put a guard on my mouth
as long as the wicked are in my presence.'

2   I held my peace and was silent;
I refrained from speaking,
but my pain disturbed me.

3   My heart within me grew hot,
fire blazed as I mused;
I spoke with my tongue:

4   'Tell me, Lord, my end,
and what the number of my days will be;
let me know how transient I am.

5   For you have certainly made my days a mere handbreadth,
and my life-span is as nothing in your sight;
all humans are indeed but a breath.

6   As a mere semblance lives a man;
aimlessly do men bustle about collecting riches,
and do not know who will inherit them.

7   But now, Lord, what is my hope?
Is it not truly you?

8   Deliver me from those who oppose me;

do not make me the butt of fools.

9 I kept silent and did not open my mouth,
for it was your doing.

10 Take away your punishment from me;
I am exhausted by the blows of your hand.

11 You discipline a man with rebukes for his sin,
and make his beauty fade like a moth;
all humans are indeed but a breath.

12 Hear my prayer, Lord,
give ear to my cry,
do not be deaf to my tears.
For I am an exile with you,
a passing stranger as were all my fathers.

13 Look away from me that I may smile
before I depart and am no more.'

The psalmist's reticence to speak offensive words against even the wicked stands in sharp contrast with modern practice. Whatever else we may consider to be wrong, generating, repeating or listening to gossip about other people is not included. Yet the biblical tradition has a different view, and in addition to the opening words of Psalm 39 we could add Job's fear that one of his children might have cursed God inadvertently, or Qoheleth's advice to say little in the presence of God (Job 1.5; Ecclesiastes 5.1). One of the hard sayings of Jesus condemns to hell fire anyone who calls someone else a fool (Matthew 5.22). Even if constrained by a convention unfamiliar to us, the psalmist is unable to contain his feelings and bursts into speech. However, his outpouring is not, as might be expected from verse 1, directed against the wicked, but against the shortness of human life and the nothingness of humans as compared with God. This makes sense if he is thinking along the following lines. If human life is so short and uncertain and if God is so real and enduring in comparison, why is it that the wicked appear to go unpunished by God? The believer suffers under a double burden, that of being taunted by fools who do not care for God (verse 8) and of having no opportunity in a fleetingly short life of experiencing any reward for faithfulness to God. Indeed, the matter is made worse by the psalmist's feeling that his own misdoings are, in fact, punished by God (verses 10–11). The psalmist's prayer, that God will give him some respite or token of encouragement before he dies (verse 13) is grounded in the thought that he can rely on the hospitality of God in the way that travellers are granted hospitality in the ancient world (verse 12). Transitory human life itself can be thought of in this way, and the history of the psalmist's own people is that of travellers such as Abraham depending upon hospitality in their journeyings in obedience to God.

The lack of belief in an afterlife in the Old Testament is often contrasted unfavourably with Christian and later Jewish belief in life after death. Yet this lack makes even more remarkable the psalmist's exclamation that his hope is in God (verse 7). In some way not indicated in the psalm, the psalmist's tradition, or his experiences in worship, had given him such a sense of the transcendent reality of God (against which he measured his own frailty) that he could hold on to this as his ultimate hope in spite of the things that distressed him. We are left wondering whether his lack of belief in an afterlife was such a disadvantage after all.

Psalm 42

1   As a deer longs for water-filled streams,
    so my soul longs for you, O God.
2   My soul thirsts for God, for the living God;
    when shall I come and see God's face?
3   Tears have been my only food day and night,
    while I am asked all day long 'Where is your God?'
4   What I remember as I pour out my soul
    is how I used to join the crowds processing to the house of
        God
    amidst shouts of joy and praise; the clamour of pilgrims.

5   Why are you bowed down, my soul,
    and distressed within me?
    Hope in God, for I will praise him yet,
    my deliverer and my God.

6   My soul is bowed down within me;
    therefore I will remember you from the land of the Jordan
        and the Hermon hills,
    from the hill of Mizar.

7   Deep calls to deep in the roar of your waterfalls;
    all your waves and breakers pass over me.

8   The Lord will show me his unfailing love by day,
    and at night his song will be on my lips,
    a prayer to the God of my life.

9   I shall say to God, my rock,
    'Why have you forgotten me? Why must I go about like a
        mourner, oppressed by my foes?'

10 Like blows that shatter my bones are my enemies' taunts,
    as they say to me day after day,
    'Where is your God?'

11 Why are you bowed down, my soul,
    and distressed within me?
    Hope in God, for I will praise him yet,
    my deliverer and my God.

Because this psalm has a refrain in verses 5 and 11 which also comes at the end of Psalm 43, the two psalms are often treated as one composition. This may be right; but Hebrew tradition has divided them and that division will be followed here. The psalmist appears to be in exile near the sources of the river Jordan and in sight of snow-capped mount Hermon. How and why he is in exile is not stated, except that his plight is attributed by him and his enemies to the absence of God. Vindication would involve his return to Jerusalem, where he would once more be able to join the temple worshippers and come into God's presence in the temple. The psalmist's 'localization' of God will not surprise us if we recall that, for many faithful churchgoers today, *the* house of God *par excellence* is where they have always worshipped or feel at home. However, more is at stake in this psalm than the feeling that God can more easily be worshipped in Jerusalem than in the awe-inspiring landscape dominated by Mount Hermon. The psalmist has no doubt that God is the living God and that he has been and is still *his* God. The taunts of his enemies 'Where is your God?' are attacks on his faith; but they are attacks also on the integrity of God. So concerned is the psalmist with these attacks that he can hardly eat (verse 3) and he compares his longing for God with the desperate search of a thirsty deer for water during the dry summer. The spectacle of some of the waterfalls at the sources of the river Jordan fills him not with awe (the touristic admiration of spectacular features of nature is a very recent invention!) but serves to describe his feeling of being overwhelmed by his troubles. If we are honest, we shall have to admit that we rarely, if ever, experience such distress if our faith or the integrity of God are called into question.

The intensity of the psalmist's distress provides him with resources for coping with it, for he is not suffering from what we would call depression. His is a distress caused by the questioning of his fundamental beliefs, but beliefs that are so strong that they can sustain him. Still, he is only human, and he longs to *see* his vindication and that of his God. Was he vindicated? We are not told, and it is safest to assume that he was not. Indeed, as a testimony to faith and hope the psalm is arguably more valuable to us as the legacy of someone who was not publicly vindicated, than as the legacy of someone who was.

Psalm 55

1   Give ear, God, to my prayer,
       and do not hide yourself from my petition.

2   Listen to me and answer me;
      I am restless in my complaining.

3   I am distressed at the voice of the enemy,
      at the onslaught of the wicked,
      for they heap wickedness upon me
      and are vindictive in their anger.

4   My heart is in turmoil within me
      and the terrors of death have descended upon me.

5   Fear and trembling seize me,
      and I shudder uncontrollably.

6   I think 'O that I had the wings of a dove;
      I would fly away and find rest.

7   I would escape far away,
      and find refuge in the wilderness.

8   I would hasten to a refuge
      from wind and tempest.'

9   Confuse them, Lord, divide their speech;
      for I have seen violence and contention in the city.

10   Day and night they compass the city on its walls,
      and wickedness and trouble are within it.

11   Destruction is in its midst,
      and oppression and deceit are never absent from its square.

12   Surely, it was no enemy that reproached me;
      that I could have borne.
      It was not my foe that rose up against me;
      I could have hidden from him.

13   It was you, a man like me;
      my companion and best friend

14   with whom I enjoyed sweet confidences
      in the house of God.

15   Let them perish in confusion,
      let death destroy them;
      let them go down to the Grave,
      for evil is at the heart of their dwellings.

16   As for me, I will call upon God;
      the Lord will save me.

17 By evening, morning and noon-tide
   I complain and mutter aloud,
   and he will hear my voice.

18 He will ransom me,
   and give my soul peace from those who fight against me,
   for they are many who oppose me.

19 God will hear me;
   he who is enthroned from eternity
   will bring low those who cling to evil,
   who have no fear of God.

20 They lay violent hands on those who belong to God;
   they profane his covenant.

21 Their speech is smoother than butter,
   but their hearts are set on war.
   Their words are softer than oil,
   but sharper than a drawn sword.

22 Cast your burden upon the Lord;
   he himself will sustain you.
   He will never allow the righteous to stumble.

23 But you, O God, will bring them down to the deepest Pit;
   murderers and deceivers,
   they will not live out half their days.
   And I will put my trust in you.

This is a very up-to-date psalm. Cities in the ancient world, as in today's world, were centres of power and resources. For this reason they could attract and become vehicles for the ambitions of unscrupulous and immoral people. In a situation in which the unscrupulous were in control, resistance to them would inevitably bring danger and reproach upon anyone standing up for what was right. Loyalties would be stretched to breaking-point and people would switch sides.

This seems to be the situation of the psalmist living, probably, in a Jerusalem (compare verse 14) whose rulers had turned their backs on God (see verses 19–20). His witness to what was just and right brought down their anger upon him, and their threats caused him great anxiety (verses 4–5). The hardest blow, however, came from the transformation of his closest friend into his opponent. The Hebrew of verse 14 suggests that the psalmist had admitted this friend to his closest secrets. We all know that the more intimate a relationship with another person becomes, the more bitter that relationship is when it breaks down. It is not surprising that the psalmist gives voice to his deep desire to escape from his predicament (verses 6–8). Many, if not all of us, must have felt like this in regard to work, or home, or even church! We even find this very human reaction in the prayer of Jesus in the Garden of Gethsemane, 'let this cup pass from me'; and it is no accident that ancient Christian interpreters of this psalm linked the words about the friend's betrayal with the betrayal of Jesus by Judas Iscariot. But escape rarely works. Similar problems meet us on the hoped-for patch of greener grass; and escape leaves the wrong-doers in the ascendancy. To stay at one's post in the situation like that of the psalmist is an ultimate test of faith – faith, not in the sense of intellectual beliefs, but faith as a way of life that embodies values and convictions. What sustains the psalmist is his hope that God who is enthroned from eternity (verse 19) will vindicate his commitment to what is good (compare verse 22b) and will destroy the evil-doers. His advice to those who can relate to his plight is not to take the wings of a dove, but to cast their burden upon God, who will sustain them.

Psalm 56

1 Be gracious to me, O God, for men are trampling upon me;
   all day long the adversary presses upon me.
2 My enemies trample on me the whole day;
   for my adversaries are many and arrogant.
3 When I am afraid I shall put my trust in you.
4 In God, whose word I praise,

in God will I trust, and not be afraid;
what can mortal flesh do to me?

5   All day long they abuse me with words;
their only thought is how to do me evil.

6   They lie in wait for me,
they watch my movements
as they seek my life.

7   Let there be no escape for them;
bring down the nations in your anger, O God.

8   You have counted my tossing and turning;
put my tears in your bottle;
record them in your book!

9   My enemies will turn back
when I call to you;
of this I am sure, for God is on my side.

10 In God whose word I praise,
in the Lord whose word I praise,

11 in God I have put my trust, and will not fear.
What can man do to me?

12 My vows to you, O God, will I perform;
I will bring a thank-offering to you.

13 For you have saved my life from death
and my feet from falling,
that I may walk before God
in the light of the living.

'What can mortal flesh do to me?' The answer is 'quite a lot'. Tor-
ture and other brutalities were not invented in the twentieth century, even if they were perfected then. One has only to read of
the fate of the prophet Uriah (Jeremiah 26.20–3) or of the impri-
sonment of Jeremiah (Jeremiah 38.6) to appreciate that kings or
nobles in Old Testament times did not scruple to kill or silence
those whose words and actions in God's name were inconvenient.
However, physical harm or death are not the only ways in
which humans can seek to harm each other. Words can be more
hurtful than blows (verse 5) as can be an atmosphere of constant

and malicious surveillance (verse 6). All this is assuming that the psalmist's perception of his plight is accurate, a fact that it is not intended to deny. However, those who suffer from depression, for whom the smallest and the most apparently trivial things can assume gigantic proportions, may recognize in this psalm a description of their plight also.

The response of the psalmist is eschatological, that is, he views his situation from the perspective of God's completed work and the processes that lead to that completion. If the answer to the question 'What can mortal flesh do to me?' is 'quite a lot', there remains the question, 'What can God do for me, who is on my side?' The answer to that question is that God will bring him into the divine presence, to a dimension of life described by the cryptic but revealing words 'in the light of the living' or 'in the light of life' (both translations of verse 13 being possible). That must lie in the future. A part of the process that leads to that future is God's attention to the psalmist's present sufferings in the course of what is right – God's counting his tears by putting them in a flask; the recording of the psalmist's anxieties in the book. The eschatological dimension from which the psalmist views his world is provided by praise and worship. Almost as a refrain, the words 'God whose word I praise' recur in the psalm. God's word is not the Bible, which was far from complete when the psalm was composed. God's word is the received tradition about his promises and his nature, a tradition renewed and refreshed by the believing community, and made his own property by the psalmist. Thus the psalm is not only a summons to today's users of it to view their life from the dimension of God's completed work. It is also a summons to the Church to order its worship in such a way that it expresses and conveys to today's believers that eschatological dimension that is at the heart of the psalm.

Psalm 73

1 Truly God is good to Israel,
   to a people pure in heart.

2 But as for me, I had almost stumbled,
   my steps had well-nigh slipped,

3 because I was provoked to anger by the boastful,
   when I saw the prosperity of the wicked.

4 They suffer no pain
   and their bodies are whole and fat.

5 They experience no misfortune as others do;
   they are not plagued like other men.

6 Thus they wear pride like a necklace;
   they wrap themselves round with violence like a garment.

7 Their eyes peer out from podgy faces;
   they obtain all their heart's desires.

8 They mock, and speak maliciously;
   what they say from on high brings oppression.

9 Their slander is directed against heaven,
   and their tongues roam freely on earth.

10 Therefore people turn to them,
   and regard them as the fountain of knowledge.

11 They say, 'How can God know;
   does the Most High have knowledge?'

12 Such are the wicked;
   they continually prosper, and increase their wealth.

13 Have I then kept my heart pure for nothing,
   and washed my hands in innocence?

14 I have been afflicted all day long,
   and chastened every morning.

15 Yet had I continued thus to talk,
   I would have betrayed the generation of your people.

16 Then I tried to think this through,
   but it was far too heavy going,

17 until I was on my way to the house of God;

then I understood their fate.

18 You will put them in slippery places;
   you will bring them down in ruin.

19 How quickly are they desolated!
   They come to an end and perish in terror.

20 One awakes from a dream and they are gone;
   one wakes up and their reputation is soiled.

21 When my heart was embittered,
   when I was cut to the quick,

22 I was surely stupid and ignorant,
   no more intelligent than an animal.

23 For I am always with you;
   you hold me by my right hand.

24 You guide me with your counsel,
   and will take me at the end to glory.

25 Who have I in heaven but you?
   And I desire no one but you on earth.

26 My body may wear out and my mind fail,
   but you, God, are my portion for ever.

27 Those who forsake you shall perish,
   and you will destroy those who whore after other gods.

28 It is good for me to draw close to God.
   I have made the Lord God my refuge,
   that I may tell of all your works.

Modern translations such as the NRSV and REB translate the
opening words as 'Truly God is good to the upright'. This is because the Hebrew consonants meaning 'to Israel' can be re-divided
to produce 'to the upright, God'. This alternative translation affects how the psalm is viewed. If 'upright' is accepted, the psalm
deals with the familiar problem of the prosperity of the wicked
and the tribulations of the faithful, and is none the worse for
that. If 'Israel' is retained, the psalm becomes more profound. It
becomes more profound because it begins with a declaration that
God is good to Israel as a whole, Israel seen as a special people,
meant to be pure in heart. To restrict God's goodness simply to

the pure in heart as a righteous element within Israel is to ignore the fact that much of the Old Testament is about God's dealing with the whole people, including those elements within it that are indifferent or hostile to God's dealings.

Viewed in this way, the psalm wrestles not so much with the problem of the prosperity of the wicked and the tribulations of the faithful, as with the question how the chosen people can come to contain individuals who view God so arrogantly, and are so contemptuous of their fellow human beings. If God is so good to Israel, why is there not a better response? The problem is one that is wrestled with not only in Psalm 73 but in the story of the wilderness wanderings in Exodus and Numbers, where the very generation of those released from slavery complain against God and Moses, and wish that they had never been freed!

Part of the answer to this question is that, as human beings, we do not like to be dependent and we certainly do not like to admit to being dependent! We like to do things our own way, and we admire others who have seemingly got to the top by their own efforts. What price other people have to pay for this success is rarely considered.

As so often in the Psalms, the viewpoint of the psalmist is not without exaggeration. It may seem to him that the wicked never have any pains or misfortunes, but is this really so? And may the psalmist not exaggerate his own difficulties? This is what makes the Psalms so endearing: the honest way in which they exaggerate in ways that we often copy.

What, then, of the Psalmist's 'solution' to his dilemma; his insight gained in, or on the way to, the sanctuary? Here, again, it is important to place the psalm in the context of God's love to Israel and not to individualize it. If we individualize it the 'solution' becomes almost the wishful thinking of one Israelite. If we retain the corporate dimension, the psalmist's 'solution' is mediated by the whole weight of the narrative and prophetic traditions of the Old Testament. The wicked act as they do because they have ignored those traditions that speak of God's justice as well as his mercy. Their contemptuous 'How can God know?'

ignores the prophetic 'Thus says the Lord'. But along with the corporate dimension is an intensely personal one. The psalmist is convinced of the love of God for him, and that this love which guides his right hand will retain its hold even to death and beyond (verse 24).

If, for Israel (verse 1), we substitute the Church and churches that we know, the psalm becomes immediately relevant. The Church exists only by the goodness of God; but its history contains episodes of power, greed and persecution. Even in our local church we may find practices and attitudes that seem to have little to do with the spirit and teaching of Jesus; and this will be because people have ceased to attend to those prophetic and narrative traditions of the Bible that record centuries of encounters with God, and which help us to see things in the light of eternity.

Psalm 88

1   O Lord God of my salvation,
      I have cried day and night before you,
2   let my prayer come into your presence;
      bend your ear to my fervent plea.
3   For my soul has had its full share of troubles
      and my life has come close to death.
4   I am thought to belong with those who go down to the pit;
      I have become a man who can no longer be helped.
5   People include me with the dead,
      like the slain who lie in the grave,
      whom you remember no longer
      and who are cut off from your hand.
6   You have put me in the lowest pit;
      in dark places and in watery depths.
7   Your anger lies heavily upon me

and your breakers have buffeted me.

8 You have removed my friends far from me,
and made me an abomination in their sight.
I am imprisoned and cannot get free.

9 My eyesight fails because of my troubles.
I have called to you, Lord, day by day;
I have stretched out my hands to you.

10 Do you work miracles for the dead?
Do the shades rise again and praise you?

11 Is your unfailing love spoken of in the grave?
Or your faithfulness in the place of destruction?

12 Are your miracles made known in the darkness,
or your saving acts in the land where all is forgotten?

13 As for me, I will cry to you, Lord,
and my prayer will come before you in the morning.

14 Why, Lord, do you spurn me?
Why do you hide your face from me?

15 I have been plagued with troubles
and wearied from my youth;
I have borne your terrors and am at my wit's end.

16 Your fierce anger has come upon me,
your terrors have destroyed me;

17 they have encircled me like a flood all day long;
they have surrounded me on every side.

18 You have removed far from me my neighbours and those I
love;
instead of companionship I have only darkness.

This is undoubtedly the saddest psalm in the whole Psalter, and
unlike some other laments it contains no concluding verses in
which the mood changes from darkness to light. Another feature
of the psalm is that it ascribes the psalmist's plight entirely to
God. It is true that part of the trouble is the judgement of neighbours and family that the psalmist is beyond help (verses 4–5),
but even this is because God has brought him to this condition
(compare verses 8, 16–18). A cynic might say that the psalm

contains an exaggerated list of tribulations, which is used as a kind of blackmail to get God to respond to the psalmist's pleas. But if we do not follow this line we have to ask what spiritual value a composition can possibly have that is almost entirely complaint.

One answer might be that the psalmist is mistaken in attributing all his troubles to God; that he is bound to be affected by human actions and agencies in a world that is unredeemed. Yet this approach only masks the fact that if people are going to believe in one supreme God, he must ultimately be held responsible for the unredeemed nature of the world; for the fact that he does not restrain the evil committed by some humans against others; that even if we escape illness in our youth (compare verse 15) it is likely to catch up with us sooner or later until it brings us to death's door (verses 3–4), and faces us with the unanswerable question of what, if anything, lies beyond the grave (verses 10–12). Looked at in this way, the psalm presents the human dilemma in the starkest possible way. To be human is to be limited: limited in terms of mental and physical health, limited in terms of life-span, limited by the impossibility of life without the love and companionship of others (verse 18). And if God is responsible for all this, it is hard to disagree with the writer of Ecclesiastes when he says that life is 'an unhappy business that God has given human beings to be busy with' (Ecclesiastes 1.13).

But is this true? Was there *no* joy *ever* in the psalmist's life? Was there *nothing* on which he could look back with pleasure? The fact that he could regret the loss of companionship (verse 18) suggests that there had been lighter moments in his life and that the unrelieved pessimism of the psalm was a one-sided interpretation.

But it would be wrong to dismiss the psalm as inadequate on the grounds that it overlooks the joys that the psalmist must have had. If this were done it would also be necessary to dismiss psalms that concentrate on joys to the exclusion of sorrows (e.g. psalms 125; 128). The fact is that part of our limitation as human beings is a tendency to be overwhelmed by the concerns of the moment, and if these are troublesome the result will be pessimism.

The psalm indicates that, depending on circumstances and how we feel, our experience of God may be perplexing as well as liberating. Further, this perplexity may be far more common than is generally appreciated. By including Psalm 88 in the Psalter, its editors have been scrupulously honest in indicating what faith in God may sometimes bring us to. That honesty could well be the first glimmer of light that persuades us that the psalm is not the whole truth about our dealings with God, even if it accurately describes how we may sometimes feel.

2

Psalms Crying Out for Justice

Psalm 12

1 Help me, Lord, for God-fearing men are no more,
   and the faithful have vanished from human society.
2 People tell lies to each other;
   their speech is smooth
   but their heart is deceitful.
3 Would that the Lord would cut off all smooth speech,
   and tongues that boast so shamelessly,
4 that say 'Our speech will win the day,
   we can say what we like.
   Who will restrain us?'
5 'Because the poor are plundered
   and the destitute groan for help,
   I will rise at once,' says the Lord.
6 'I will make them safe from those who trouble them.'
   The words of the Lord are pure,
   like silver and gold refined seven times.
7 You will surely guard them, Lord;
   you will protect us from this evil generation for ever.
8 The wicked walk confidently on every side
   when what is worthless is esteemed among men.

This psalm describes a situation familiar in today's world, as well as in that of the psalmist. It is a world in which words become weapons in battles for political and other kinds of power. The costs of major building projects are understated, the numbers of their likely users exaggerated. Politicians comment on the results of by-elections to turn loss into triumph for themselves, and success into failure for their opponents. Constructive debate is a casualty of the need to demonstrate that any opponent has only dark and dishonest motives. Even the Internet, for all its advantages, makes information available that cannot be reviewed and corrected by experts.

The way that words are used is a pointer to several things. It is a pointer to the kind of arrogance displayed in verse 4, the arrogance of those who are a law unto themselves and who will stop at nothing to get their own way. But the use, or rather misuse, of words can bring despair to anyone who cares for the truth, and for its practical application in justice (compare verse 5). The complaint of the opening verse to the effect that integrity has entirely vanished, and the observation of the last verse that only what is worthless is esteemed, are expressions of the way many people feel in today's world. It is no surprise that so few people bother to vote in elections, given the sense that politics is at best irrelevant and at worst corrupt. The real tragedy is when ordinary people come to feel that there are few others whom they can genuinely trust in life (verse 1).

The psalmist contrasts the esteeming of what is worthless by the wicked (verse 8) with God's words that are like purely refined silver and gold (verse 6); but what does this mean? The reference in verse 6 is not to the Bible, which did not exist as such when the psalm was composed. The reference is not necessarily to the promise in verse 5 that God will immediately act to rescue the poor and destitute. After all, the Psalms often complain about God's apparent failure to act in this way. A possible answer is that the psalm articulates the deep human longing for something greater than which cannot be thought or imagined, an ultimate source of truth and constancy that contrasts with human frailty and its cynical manipulation of words and truth for sectional interests. This longing for truth and constancy is a profound religious experience, and faith made possible by God grasps the hope that it is the ultimate reality. To discover this in this world, however, entails that we are tested and refined in our conflicts with all that is false and worthless. Only thus do we discover that God's promises are like purified silver and gold.

Psalm 36

1   The wicked man proclaims the wickedness deep in his heart;
there is no fear of God in his eyes.

2   He flatters himself in his own sight
and hates his wrong-doing to be known.

3   He speaks only wickedness and lies;
he has ceased to act wisely or to do good.

4   He makes evil plans as he lies abed,
he takes his stand on a path that is not good,
and nothing that is evil will he reject.

5   Your unfailing love, Lord, reaches to the heavens,
and your faithfulness to the clouds.

6   Your righteous judgement is like the high mountains,
your justice like the great deep.
You save both man and beast, O Lord;

7   how precious is your unfailing love, O God!
The children of men will take refuge
under the shadow of your wings.

8   They will be filled with the plenty of your house
and you will quench their thirst from the river of your
delights.

9   For with you is the well of life,
and in your light we shall see light.

10   Maintain your unfailing love to those who know you,
and your righteous judgement to those who are upright of
heart.

11   Do not let the foot of the proud come near me,
nor let the hand of the wicked push me away.

12 Those who act wickedly have fallen;
    they are brought down and will not be able to rise.

The opening verse of this psalm is difficult to translate, as a comparison of modern versions will indicate. The first word, the Hebrew $n^e um$, means 'oracle' and is common in the prophetic books in its rendering 'says the Lord' (literally, 'oracle of the Lord') at the end of divine speeches. In Psalm 36 it is used for utterances of the wicked, perhaps indicating their brazen arrogance. Indeed, this is a psalm that is painted in black and white colours, with no room for grey. The wicked are really wicked. They are opinionated, unwilling to admit being in the wrong, constantly planning evil, and committed to a way of life that is dedicated to evil. That is the black.

The white is not, as one might expect, the unimpeachable character of a god-fearing person, but the character of God himself. The divine qualities that are stressed are faithfulness, fair dealing and justice, and the things that they are compared with imply that they permeate the whole universe (verses 5–6). Such is their scope that they extend to animals as well as humans (verse 6c), implying God's concern to save the former from cruel exploitation by the wicked. The wicked presumably act as they do because they know what they want and will stop at nothing to get it. God also has things on offer, and there is even a hint of a heavenly banquet in verse 8. True life and light have only one source (verse 9).

The real world is different, of course, with its various shades of grey, and with wickedness adopting many guises of plausibility. Occasionally, in the brutalities of war and the inhumanity of dictatorships we glimpse wickedness in its true colours, and are appalled. The value of Psalm 36 is precisely its unwillingness to recognize the shades of grey and the compromises that underlie them, even though there must have been as many shades of grey in the psalmist's world as there are in ours. This is an eschatological psalm in the sense that it views the world from the perspective of God's triumph over evil (verse 12), the triumph that shows wickedness up for what it is. Nevertheless, the psalmist, like us, has to live in a world where God's triumph over evil is neither complete nor obvious. This is why he has to pray for God's continuing mercy and protection (verses 10–11); and no doubt he, like us, also prayed that the compromises with evil, that are a necessary part of daily life, would not blur his vision of a better world, so nobly described in verses 5–9.

Psalm 58

1 You mighty, do you really dispense justice?
   Do you judge your fellow-citizens fairly?
2 No. You deliberately perpetrate wicked deeds in the land;
   your hands mete out violence.
3 The wicked go their own way from the womb;
   from birth they are erring liars.
4 Their rage is like the venom of serpents;
   they are like the deaf adder that blocks its ears,
5 so that it does not hear the voice of the charmers
   however skilled at casting spells.
6 Smash their teeth, God, in their mouths;
   break the jaws of these young lions, Lord.
7 Let them drain away like water hither and thither;
   let them be trodden down and wither like grass;
8 let them be like a trail left by a snail,
   like a woman's miscarriage that does not see the sun.
9 Before they know it let their thorns blaze like fuel,
   like green thorns which are swept fiercely away.
10 The righteous will rejoice when he sees vengeance;
   he will bathe his feet in the blood of the wicked,
11 and men will say 'The righteous has a reward;
   there is indeed a God who judges in the earth.'

The interpretation of this psalm depends crucially upon the obscure Hebrew word in verse 1 *'êlem*. The PBV and AV translated it as 'congregation' in dependence on the great medieval Jewish grammarian and lexicographer David Qimhi; but Qimhi understood the psalm to have been spoken by David against Abner, Saul's commander, and other members of Saul's entourage, when they accused David of rebelling against Saul. Christian interpreters referred the psalm to Christ on the cross, with those accused in the psalm being the Jews who crucified him. The RV translators took *'êlem* to mean 'silence', with the RV margin giving the rendering 'is the righteousness ye should speak dumb?', the implication being that judges are addressed who are silent instead of condemning what is wrong.

Because the three consonants *'e l m* form the basis of the Hebrew words for God, *'el* and *'elohim*, modern scholars have taken the word to be a reference to gods or, in accordance with Job 41.25 (Hebrew 41.17), a reference to the mighty, and this is what is done in the above translation. This yields a coherent interpretation, and makes the psalm one of accusation and hoped-for judgement against those in power and authority who abuse their trust. Verses 3–5 give an unflattering portrait of the compromised rulers. From birth they are estranged, that is, the ways of goodness are foreign to them, and lying is second nature from the beginning. However, there is no sense here of 'original sin'. The image of the deadly snake whose bite is fatal, and the deaf adder which can resist the most skilled charmer, can hardly be bettered as poetic descriptions of opinionated people whose decisions can ruin the lives of ordinary citizens.

Verses 6–9 continue the powerful poetry in expressing what the psalmist hopes for the corrupt rulers. The images are self-explanatory, but the translation offered follows modern commentators in reading *hatsir* 'grass' instead of *hitsav* 'his arrows' in verse 7b. The allusion in verse 9 is to the wind, which can blow so fiercely in the desert that the fuel (thorns or brambles) is either blown away completely or is exhausted before a pot is properly warmed. The final two verses express the future hope that when God's judgement has been executed upon these rulers, there will be general rejoicing on the part of all people of good will.

Psalm 58 is a psalm that has been deemed by the Church of England to be unsuitable for public worship in its entirety. No doubt the description in verse 10 of the righteous bathing their feet in the blood of the wicked has contributed to this, and it is also possible to mock at the 'deaf adder that blocks its ears'. Yet this last phrase is vividly poetic and expressive, and gory though bathing feet in blood may be, it captures well the revulsion that is felt against injustice and corruption in high places. No doubt the psalm also exaggerates in verse 3 in suggesting that the corrupt are like this from their birth. The sad truth is that power can insidiously corrupt people who set out with the best of intentions; but again, it must not be forgotten that the Psalms are poetry.

Corruption in high places is alas as much a feature of life today as it was in ancient Israel. Recent scandals have implicated leaders in the United States, Germany and Israel, not to mention accusations of 'sleaze' and perjury against politicians in Britain. Scandals such as these bring with them despair and cynicism, and destroy faith in justice and in the political system. They are a reminder that those in power, like those of us who are ordinary citizens, are fallible and potentially corruptible human beings. Used in the right way and in the right context, Psalm 58 is not an embarrassment but a psalm that touches upon human despair and human hope in a profound way. It can be prayed by all who are appalled at injustice in high places and all who hope for God's perfect rule; and it can serve as a prayer that, through the grace of God, we may have the strength and courage to be scrupulously honest in all our own dealings, especially as they affect the lives of others.

Psalm 61

1   Hear, O God, my cry,
      give ear to my prayer.

2   From the ends of the earth I call to you
    when my heart faints.
    Set me on a rock that is higher than me.
3   For you have been my refuge,
    a strong tower against the enemy.
4   I will dwell in your tent for ever
    and shelter under the cover of your wings!
5   You indeed, O God, have heard my vows;
    you have granted the desire of those who revere your name.
6   May you add many days to the life of the king;
    may his years span the generations.
7   May he be enthroned for ever in God's presence;
    may constant love and truth be his protection.
8   Thus will I ever sing praise to your name,
    and fulfil my vows day by day.

As a welcome contrast to psalms that ascribe the psalmist's troubles to his conflicts with those in power, Psalm 61 contains a prayer for the well-being of the king. This is a reminder that although power can corrupt, it can also be used creatively and beneficially. All of us who have power, in whatever way, need this reminder – not least in the churches! Also lacking in the psalm is a description of oppression that results from the psalmist's loyalty to God. Evidently, the king's reign ensures that the psalmist can fulfil his religious obligations without hindrance; and this state of affairs is seen as an indication of God's blessing (verses 5, 8). However, it is sometimes less easy to be faithful to God when all is going well than when hostility has to be faced. The sharp dividing line between black and white so evident in a psalm such as Psalm 56 can become blurred. If all is right with the world, is there any need for God? The answer to that question is 'no', if God is merely seen as a last resort when all else has failed in the face of difficulties. The answer is 'yes' if God has been encountered as a transcendent reality who gives sense and purpose in an otherwise ambiguous world. The opening verses of the psalm certainly express the psalmist's sense of God as an abiding reality in contrast to the psalmist's frailty. God's presence extends to ends of the earth (verse 2), he can provide a rock higher than the psalmist; the psalmist can count on the hospitality and protection of God (verse 4) as a stranger in a foreign land would hope to be protected by its inhabitants. It is because the psalmist has this sense of God's reality that he does not take for granted the favourable conditions fostered by the king, but prays that God will continue them. This, then, is a psalm for good times, times that call for thanksgiving and prayer.

Psalm 82

1   God takes his place in the council of heaven,
     he judges in the assembly of gods.
2   'How long will you judge unjustly
     and favour the cause of the wicked?
3   Judge rather the poor and fatherless,
     do justice to the needy and oppressed.
4   Deliver the poor and needy;
     save them from the power of the wicked.'
5   They neither know nor understand;
     they walk in darkness.
     The foundations of the earth are shaken.
6   My sentence is as follows:
     'You are gods,
     all of you sons of the Most High.
7   However, you shall die like humans
     and fall like a human prince.'
8   Rise up, O God, judge the earth,
     for you shall have possession of all the nations.

The probable background to this psalm is the belief found in passages such as Deuteronomy 32.8–9 that each nation in the world has a heavenly being to look after it, Israel being the particular concern of God himself. The image of a heavenly court over which God presides is familiar from the prologue to the Book of Job as well as 1 Kings 22.19–22. It was no doubt inspired by earthly royal courts, and in later Judaism and in Christianity supplied the locale for named angels and archangels. In the psalm God summons the heavenly beings that have charge of the nations, and accuses them of corruption and of failing to defend the poor. He passes sentence on them: they will lose their divine status and suffer the fate of ordinary mortals. The psalm ends with a plea to God to arise in judgement, and to take over responsibility for the nations that have been failed by their heavenly guardians. It is possible, of course, that behind this psalm there is a religious struggle, a struggle to banish all gods and types of religion, other than that of Israel's official worship.

A question that must be asked is whether the condemned heavenly beings have been fairly treated. If the nations over whom they watched were incapable of maintaining justice, cannot the same be said of Israel? If the heavenly beings are to be made responsible for the failures of their charges, cannot the same blame be laid at the door of Israel's God? If God is to take over responsibility for all the nations (verse 8) is this such good news after all?

The question could be softened by taking the view that only human judges are being condemned in verses 2–4, although this hardly makes sense of the sentence passed on them. Another view is that foreign rulers oppressing Israel are being referred to; however, it is best to take the most difficult approach.

The question is that of ultimate responsibility. Where does true justice come from; how can it be ensured? That this is a practical and important matter needs no justification in Britain, where there have been too many instances of the Court of Appeal having to quash the sentences of people imprisoned, in some cases for many years, to allow us to believe that our system of justice is free from error or corruption. The psalm is saying that justice cannot be guaranteed by humankind, nor even by heavenly beings. Only the ultimate source of truth and justice, the God we worship, can give that guarantee; and it will not be found in the as yet unredeemed world of our experience.

Psalm 94

1   O Lord, God who avenges wrongs,
       God who avenges wrongs, make yourself known.

2   Rise up, judge of the earth;
       reward the proud as they deserve.

3   How long, Lord,
       how long will the wicked exult?

4   They spout forth arrogant words;
       the evil-doers boast proudly.

5   They crush your people, Lord,
       and oppress the ones you have chosen.

6   They murder the widows and strangers,
       and put the fatherless to death.

7   They say 'Yah will not see.
       The God of Jacob will not notice.'

8   Take note of this, you senseless among the people.
       You fools, when will you understand?

9   Cannot he who planted the ear hear?
       Cannot he who formed the eye see?

10   Will not he who guides the nations punish them?
       Is the teacher of mankind ignorant?

11   The Lord knows the thoughts of man,
       that they are wind.

12   Happy is the man whom you correct;
       whom you instruct out of your law,

13   giving him respite from days of badness
       until a pit is dug for the wicked.

14 For the Lord will not forsake his people,
nor abandon those he has chosen.

15 For justice will once more be administered rightly,
and all who are true in heart will be glad.

16 Who will stand up for me against the wicked?
Who will stand by me against evil-doers?

17 If the Lord had not been my helper
I would soon have been put to silence.

18 But when I said 'My foot has slipped',
your unfailing love, Lord, held me up.

19 In all the perplexity of my mind,
your consolations gave me joy.

20 Can those who cover up their wickedness have you as an ally,
those who produce evil by passing laws?

21 They band themselves against the life of the righteous,
and condemn the innocent to death.

22 But the Lord is with me as a stronghold,
and my God is the rock in whom I trust.

23 He will make their wickedness rebound on them,
and destroy them for their evil doing;
the Lord our God will destroy them.

This remarkable psalm suggests a situation in which corruption in the life of the nation has reached the point where the rulers and judges not only deny justice to innocent people, especially if they are poor and defenceless (verse 6), but also use their power to pass laws that are unjust (verse 20). There is even a possible example of their blasphemous speech in verse 7, where they use the rare, and probably shortened form of Yahweh, Yah, to refer to God. Since in compositions such as Exodus 15 and Psalm 68 the name Yah is associated with God's mighty acts of deliverance, its use in this psalm may be deliberate irony, meaning that the mighty deliverer of the past is powerless to do anything in the present. Situations such as that implied in the psalm are regularly described and condemned in the prophetic books. A particularly strong expression is found in Micah 3.19–10 where the rulers of Jerusalem are condemned

> who abhor justice
> and pervert all equity,
> who build Zion with blood
> and Jerusalem with wrong!

Similar situations may well face believers today in local and national government, and in local and national churches.

The psalmist addresses these corrupt rulers and lawmakers with an intellectual argument, based on creation, that is still not without force. Can it really be that the God who created ears and eyes is himself blind and deaf to injustice? If his creatures at their best are scandalized by corruption and falsehood, can God remain indifferent to these things? In his perplexity (verse 19) the psalmist assures himself that God can never be an ally of such corruption, whereas the psalmist in prayer and worship enjoys the assurance of God's unfailing love.

There is also, however, an opportunity to consider a question raised by Karl Barth in his commentary on the Letter to the Romans. Commenting on Romans 12.20, 'never avenge yourselves, but leave it to the wrath of God', Barth ponders the dilemma of anyone who, seeing injustice going unpunished, is tempted to act on behalf of God.

Shall I take the matter into my own hands? Shall I undertake to battle for the right? Shall I become myself the invisible God? ... Who will pronounce judgement upon me if I do this? ... What else could I do in the presence of the enemy but, as the representative of the absent God, advance against him with word and deed, with the force of law and of arms, with the whole offensive and defensive might of the world? ... it is in the enemy that the righteousness of God is represented as something altogether distant from us, as something strange and undo-able. In the enemy the righteousness of God appears only as His wrath, and God Himself is revealed to us as – Deus absconditus.

(K. Barth, *The Epistle to the Romans*, translated by E. C. Hoskins, London: Oxford University Press, 1933, pp. 472, 474; German original *Der Römerbrief* (Zweite Fassung 1922), Zürich: Theologischer Verlag, 1999, pp. 497–8; pp. 456, 458 in the 6th original edition.)

This remarkable passage is the more interesting because, both in the Old Testament and in recent events in Europe and elsewhere, there are, and have been, instances in which concerted civil action has swept away corrupt rulers and their regimes. And yet, as Barth reminds us, as soon as we usurp the place of the apparently absent God and take the avenging of wrongs into our own hands, we run the danger of reducing God to a projection of our own concerns, a God who is there to support *our* country, *our* church, *our* theology. The God of the Psalms, who is apparently absent from the world, or indifferent to injustice, is the living, sovereign God, far removed from our petty concerns, but yet the one who calls us his sons and daughters and surrounds us with his unfailing love. What this psalm teaches us is that we must always be sensitive to corruption and injustice, that we must always seek to denounce it and, where necessary, take action to bring it to an end. But we must never do this as those who believe that we can ultimately achieve and complete God's own work. That was possibly how some, at least, of the corrupt rulers and judges began!

3

The Penitential Psalms

Psalm 6

1   Lord, do not correct me in your anger,
    nor discipline me because of your fierce displeasure.

2   Have mercy on me, Lord,
    for I am frail; heal me, Lord, for my bones are dismayed.

3   My soul also is greatly disturbed,
    and as for you, Lord,
    how long must I wait?

4   Turn to me, Lord, deliver my soul,
    save me in accordance with your unfailing love.

5   For among the dead no one remembers you;
    in the grave who can give you thanks?

6   I am worn out with my groaning;
    every night I flood my bed with tears
    and dissolve my couch in my weeping.

7   My eyesight fails from grief,
    and is worn out because of my enemies.

8   Depart from me all you evil-doers,
    for the Lord has heard the voice of my weeping.

9   The Lord has heard my plea for favour,
    he accepts my prayer.

10 All my enemies shall be put to great shame and distress;
    they shall turn back and be suddenly confounded.

The most striking thing about this psalm is its sudden change of mood, from anguished petition in verses 1–7, to confident affirmation in the last three verses. Scholars have sometimes explained this as the psalmist's response to a word of blessing or assurance, spoken by a priest or cultical official before the change of mood, but not recorded in the text of the psalm. However, there is a less obvious, deeper, and more important contrast in the psalm that must be noticed, and which fundamentally affects its interpretation. Verses 1–7a are a dialogue between the psalmist and God. The psalmist's enemies are not mentioned until verse 7b and as soon as they are mentioned they are rebuked, because the psalmist is confident that God is with him. What this means is that the first seven verses are not the sentiments of someone from whom God is absent, while the concluding verses indicate a recovery of God's favour; the first seven verses are uttered within the context of a trusting relationship with God.

The Bible has numerous examples of individuals arguing with God about the way he appears to run, or not to run, the world. The Book of Job contains many such instances, as does the Psalter; and it is one of the abiding values of the Old Testament that it describes people interrogating God. What this implies can be illustrated if we imagine that we are on familiar terms with a famous or very important person, perhaps because we are related to them or studied under them. While we in no way belittle their importance, because of our relationship with them we can say things that other people would never dare or contemplate. It is in this spirit that the psalmist can rebuke the evil-doers.

He opens the psalm, then, by acknowledging the distance between God and himself. God's anger and displeasure would annihilate the psalmist. He needs God's mercy because of his frailty. But his relationship with God is such that he can question why God does not appear to act, and can even remind God of the widespread belief that death brought any intimate connection with God to an end (verse 5). This view is, of course, questioned elsewhere in the Psalms (e.g. 139.8), but it is important in this psalm because death will mean the termination of the psalmist's relationship with God, not just the end of his own physical existence. The psalm takes us, then, beyond the simplistic calculus in which God is no more than a device for enabling the psalmist to get his own way. In dealings with other human beings and God, friendship becomes a dimension in which things can be said that would not be possible in other circumstances, and where the processes of calculating advantage have no place.

Psalm 32

1 Happy the one whose transgression is forgiven,
 whose sin is pardoned.

2 Happy the man to whom the Lord imputes no guilt,
 in whose spirit is no guile.

3 While I kept silent
 my bones were eaten away
 by my daily groaning in distress;

4 for your hand weighed heavily upon me day and night,
 my strength dried up as in a summer drought.

5 I acknowledged my sin to you
 and have not concealed my iniquity;
 I said: 'I will confess to the Lord my transgressions'
 and you forgave the wickedness of my sin.

6 Therefore let every faithful one
 pray to you when you may be found;
 a flood of mighty waters shall not reach him.

7 You are a hiding-place for me;
 you will protect me from trouble,
 you will surround me with shouts of deliverance.

8 I will instruct you and direct you
 in the path you should take;
 I will keep my eye on you and give you good advice.

9 Do not be like horse or mule that do not understand;
 who are held back by bit and bridle
 from coming close to you.

10 Many are the tribulations that come upon the wicked;
 but unfailing love surrounds whoever trusts in the Lord.

11 Rejoice in the Lord and be glad you righteous;
    let all who are upright in heart shout for joy.

We who are so used to hearing the absolution pronounced in our
church services without this making very much difference to us,
may find it hard to empathize with this psalm. What it seems to
be about is the lifting of a great burden, the sudden opening up
of a future unclouded by the present or the past. The psalm
does not begin at the beginning. The beginning was the point at
which, for whatever reason, the psalmist felt unable to unburden
himself before God, and this self-imposed silence became a
cancer at the heart of his physical as well as spiritual well-being
(verses 3–4).

Why should the psalmist have been reluctant to unburden himself before God? Did he feel that his misdeeds were so foul that
they were beyond redemption? Did he feel that, from God's perspective, they were too trivial to deserve attention? Did he not
know how to find his way to God? Whatever the reason, the
psalmist was able to experience a profound release from his
burden of guilt, and this occasioned his outburst in the two opening verses. From these it is apparent not only that he felt
pardoned, but that this experience meant that he did not want to
try to conceal anything from God (verse 2b).

Such was the force of his experience that it made him a mission-
ary, commending to others that they, too, should seek God
(verse 6). If the mighty waters of verse 6 are not literal floods
but a poetic description of troubles in general, the psalmist is
saying that the experience of God's forgiveness will provide
powerful resources for coping with difficulties. The same point
is made in verse 7.

The identity of the speaker of verses 8–9 is not easy to determine. If it is God addressing the psalmist he is saying, in effect,
how silly the psalmist was not to have unburdened himself
sooner, and that God will gladly direct his path from now on. If
the psalmist is the speaker, he is addressing his fellow believers.
Verse 9 is particularly difficult, and the translation given here

could well be wrong. Some versions render it to mean that the horse and mule will only follow a man if they are led by bit and bridle. Whether it is fair, to horses at least, to describe them as not understanding will no doubt be disputed by horse-lovers.

It is easy for today's users of the psalm to adopt a superior attitude to the psalmist, and to feel that he was at best ill advised to be reluctant to approach God. That is because we are rarely in a situation when we are overburdened with guilt. Obviously, we do not want, or need, to develop guilt-complexes for the sake of it. Nonetheless, if we do find it difficult to empathize with the psalm this may be because we have become too sensitized to evil; and there is the distressing fact that the forms of confession that we use in the Church of England are all framed in terms of individual wrong-doing, with no sense of our involvement in and responsibility for the corporate and structural wrongs of the world. Perhaps a good way into using the psalm is to think of precisely this corporate dimension of wrong.

Psalm 35

1   Defend my cause, Lord,
     against those who oppose me;
     make war against those who fight me.
2   Take hold of shield large and small,
     and rise up to help me.
3   Draw the spear,
     and bar the way to those who pursue me.
     Say to me, 'I am your deliverer.'
4   Let those who seek my life
     be put to shame or derision.
     Let them be turned back and put to shame
     who plan evil against me.
5   Let them be like chaff blown away by the wind,
     driven by an angel of the Lord.

6   May their path be dark and slippery,
    pursued by an angel of the Lord.

7   For they have secretly spread out a net for me
    for no good cause,
    and for no good cause
    they have dug a pit for me.

8   Let ruin come upon them unawares;
    the net that they have hidden catch them.
    May they fall into their pit!

9   Let me rejoice in the Lord,
    and be glad in his deliverance.

10 All my bones will say:
    Lord, who is like you,
    who delivers the poor
    from one too strong for him,
    the poor and needy from
    one who would despoil him?

11 False witnesses stand up against me;
    I am questioned about things I do not know.

12 They repay me good for evil,
    making me feel bereaved.

13 For my part, when they were sick,
    I wore sackcloth;
    I denied myself with fasting,
    even though my prayer came back unanswered.

14 I behaved as though they were my friend or brother;
    as one mourns his mother
    I was bowed down with grief.

15 But when I stumbled they were filled with glee and ganged up –
    yes, ganged up on me.
    Like strangers I never knew,
    they attacked me unceasingly.

16 When I slipped they mocked me mercilessly;
    they ground their teeth in rage against me.

17 Lord, how long will you merely look on?
    Rescue my life from the evil they plan.

Deliver me from the lions.

18 I will give thanks to you in the great congregations.
I will praise you before mighty throngs.

19 Let not my enemies who love falsehood triumph over me,
nor those who hate me for no reason mock me.

20 It is not peace that they talk about,
but disturbing the land;
they invent lies and rumours.

21 They jeer at me, saying, 'Aha, aha!
We have seen what we want.'

22 But you have seen it also, Lord.
Do not be silent;
do not be far from me.

23 Arise, awake to uphold my rights;
defend my cause, my God and Lord.

24 Judge me in accordance with your justice, Lord God,
so that they do not triumph over me.

25 Let them not say in their hearts 'We have won.'
Let them not say,
'We have destroyed him.'

26 Let them be both ashamed and disgraced
who gleefully do me harm;
let them be covered with shame and dishonour,
who exalt themselves against me.

27 Let those who favour my vindication shout and be glad;
let them say continually,
'The Lord is great
who desires his servant's good.'
And my tongue will tell of your justice,
and of your praise all the day long.

If it were not for verses 1b–8 this would be a relatively easy psalm
to interpret. The opening words use the language of the law-
court; the psalmist asks God to be his advocate in a dispute.
This language is repeated in verse 23, and in the meantime the
psalmist has complained about people who bring malicious

charges against him for no apparent reason (verses 11–12). Verses 1b–8, however, use military language. The psalmist asks God to take up arms on his behalf, and to rout his enemies in the way that enemies are routed in some of the stories in Joshua, Judges and Chronicles. The alternation of legal and military language accordingly blurs the focus of the psalm.

A possible way in to the psalm for modern users is the fact that in modern, as in ancient, warfare, there are no final arbiters. Wars are won by the strongest, whether strength is measured in terms of superior military hardware, or in terms of the greater will of a nation to survive. It is true that, in the twentieth century, attempts were made to regulate warfare and to set up institutions to prosecute war criminals, but it has to be admitted that this had only limited success. In the nineteenth and earlier centuries there were no international bodies to check the colonial invasion by Britain, France, Spain, Portugal and the Netherlands of parts of Africa, the Far East, Latin and North America, India, and Australia and New Zealand. In these instances, the stronger nations were able to defeat and colonize the weaker ones. Might was right. If this line of thought is followed, it is possible to see why the psalmist asks God to fight on his behalf. If his is a just cause, it is not right that he should be defeated; but only God can ultimately assure justice, or so the psalmist believes.

The military language of verses 1b–8 does not have to be taken literally, however, if its primary purpose is to describe a situation in which only divine intervention can prevent the triumph of evil over good, of the stronger over the weaker. This can then be linked to the situation of law-courts in ancient Israel.

In today's western world we are used to judicial systems in which appeal to higher courts can be made against verdicts in lower courts. In some cases there are also European courts and the International Court of Justice at The Hague. No such appeal courts existed in ancient Israel. Although Israelite justice was a serious matter and false witnesses could suffer severe penalties for perjury (Deuteronomy 19.6–21), there is abundant evidence in the Old Testament that the scales of justice could be heavily weighted in favour of the rich and powerful. The psalm can be read as the desperate cry to God for justice on the part of an innocent person maliciously arraigned before a court. The situation is all the more bitter because the psalmist's accusers are not strangers, but people for whom he had prayed and whose plight he had sought to alleviate (verses 13–14). Elsewhere in the Old Testament it is strongly affirmed that in cases where there is no one to protect the vulnerable, God will note their plight and mete out punishment to their oppressors (see Exodus 22.21–4, 27).

To use the psalm today, it is not necessary to invoke the law-court image. There are countless situations in daily life in which the stronger prevail unjustly over the weaker, with no redress. This happens in the home, at school and at work. Also in these situations false accusations, fuelled by jealousy and ambition, can destroy the reputation and prospects of innocent people. Does God see and act? We do not know; we hope, however, that the anger that such situations arouse in us is felt by God – we hope that we are not better than God. And it lies in our power to ensure that, in situations where we are the stronger, we do not abuse that strength, and that whenever we can we stand on the side of justice against the abuse of power.

Psalm 51

1   Have mercy on me, God, according to your unfailing love;
according to the great number of your mercies
blot out my offences.

2   Wash me spotlessly clean from my wickedness,
and cleanse me from my sin.

3   I am fully aware of my offences,
and always conscious of my sin.

4   It is you alone against whom I sin
and do evil in your sight,

so that when you speak,
your sentence is just,
your judgements faultless.

5   I was brought to birth in wickedness;
my mother conceived me in sin.

6   You desire truth in hidden places,
and teach me wisdom in secret.

7   You purify me with hyssop and I am clean,
you wash me and I am whiter than snow.

8   You make me hear joy and gladness;
the bones you have broken rejoice.

9   Hide your face from my sins,
and blot out all my wrong-doings.

10   Create a clean heart in me, God,
and make new in me an upright spirit.

11   Do not cast me from your presence,
and do not take your holy spirit from me.

12   Restore to me the joy of your salvation,
and support me with a willing spirit.

13   Let me teach offenders your ways,
so that sinners return to you.

14   Save me from shedding blood, O God,
the God of my salvation.
My tongue shouts aloud your justice.

15   You open my lips,
and my mouth declares your praise.

16   For if you desired a sacrifice
I would bring it;
but you desire no burnt offering.

17   My sacrifice, O God,
is a broken spirit;
a broken and contrite heart, O God,
you will not spurn.

18   In your favour do good to Zion;
build the walls of Jerusalem.

19   Then you will take pleasure in right sacrifices,

burnt and whole offerings;
then shall bulls be offered upon your altar.

No translation can do justice to the Hebrew of this psalm, so many are its allusions to practices and institutions unfamiliar to most modern users. Its first remarkable feature is the way it describes human wrong-doing. Three key words are given in the opening two verses: 'offences', implying rebelling; 'wickedness', implying guilt; and 'sin', implying a falling short of God's requirements. These are formal acts of commission or omission; but the psalm also locates them in the inner nature of humankind, back to the very beginning of life itself (verse 5). There is, of course, no suggestion here of the Christian doctrine of original or inherited sin. It is simply that the psalmist is so aware of his failings that he is prepared to trace them back to his very birth.

Matching the account of human types of wrong-doing are words for their remedy. 'Wash me' in verses 2 and 7b is a word used for the treading and kneading of clothes to launder them in a society deficient in cleansing agents. 'Blot out' in verse 1 has the sense of removing all trace of, while 'cleanse me' in verse 2 is a verb also used in connection with purifying metals and cleansing the land or the temple from what is unclean. 'Purify' in verse 7 is a cultic word used elsewhere for purifying from uncleanness by the sprinkling of sacrificial blood.

These actions of cleansing and purifying in ancient Israel were 'external' in the sense of dealing primarily with ritual offences. The psalm recognizes a need for a deeper type of cleansing and in verses 9–11 uses terms that have moral significance. 'Create' in verse 10 is a verb usually reserved for God's creative action, as in Genesis 1.1. Here it almost suggests recreation of the individual. The heart (verse 10) is the seat of the intellect in Hebrew thought, while the spirit denotes the disposition or character of a person. In verses 10 and 12 the psalmist prays that his character may be upright and willing, ready to offer its services.

The last four verses seem to be contradictory. Having said that God desires no sacrifices other than a broken and contrite heart, the psalmist prays for Jerusalem to be rebuilt so that sacrifices can again be offered. This has led many commentators to conclude that verses 18–19 are later additions; and these verses are often bracketed or simply omitted when the psalm is used in public worship. This may well be correct; but there is no necessary contradiction between formal public ceremonies directed towards forgiving sins, and personal requests to God for forgiveness. The absolution pronounced at services today does not remove the obligation from worshippers to seek God's forgiveness in private prayers. In ancient Israel forgiveness was in any case much more of a formal, communal affair. Even if the psalmist here uses individualistic and spiritual language about sacrifice, it is unlikely that he could have envisaged, or even welcomed, a type of religion from which formal and public acts of sacrifice were excluded.

This psalm has traditionally been translated as though it refers to a particular action or situation in the past for which the psalmist seeks forgiveness. The above translation, which is arguably closer to the meaning of the admittedly enigmatic Hebrew verbal forms of the psalm, gives a more present and enduring sense. The psalmist is aware of his failure to be perfect (verses 3–6), he rejoices at what God does to forgive his sins (verses 7–8), yet he still prays for forgiveness, outwardly (verses 1–2) and inwardly (verses 10–12). These apparent contradictions reflect, in fact, the reality of the human situation before God. We have been forgiven, we are being forgiven, but we need to pray for forgiveness. The psalm is so deep and complex that we simplify its message at our peril.

Psalm 102

1 Hear my prayer, Lord;
    let my cry for help come to you.

2 Do not hide your face from me
 when I am in trouble.
 Bend your ear to me;
 when I cry out,
 hasten to answer me.

3 For my days disperse like smoke,
 and my bones are a charred and burning mass.

4 My heart is scorched, and dry like grass;
 I have become thin, abstaining from food.

5 I groan aloud,
 my bones stuck fast to my skin.

6 I am like a desert owl,
 an owl that haunts ruins.

7 I keep solitary watch,
 and am like a sparrow
 sitting alone on a housetop.

8 My enemies taunt me all day long;
 people mad at me swear oaths against me.

9 I have eaten ashes instead of bread;
 tears have mingled with my drink,

10 because of your anger and wrath;
 for you have lifted me up and thrown me down.

11 My days have shortened like a shadow
 and I am dried up like grass.

12 But you, Lord, are enthroned for ever,
 and your name is remembered from generation to generation.

13 You will rise up and have mercy on Zion,
 for the time to have mercy on her is come indeed.

14 Your servants take delight in her stones,
 and her very dust provokes our compassion.

15 The nations will fear the name of the Lord
 and all the kings of the earth your glory.

16 When the Lord builds Zion
 he will be seen in his glory.

17 He has turned to the prayer of the destitute,
   and has not spurned their request.
18 This should be written for a later generation,
   and people yet to be born will praise the Lord.
19 For he looks down from his holy height,
   from heaven the Lord looks upon earth,
20 to hear the groaning of the prisoner,
   to set free those condemned to death.
21 The Lord's name will be proclaimed in Zion,
   and his praise in Jerusalem,
22 when peoples are gathered together
   and kingdoms come to serve the Lord.
23 He has reduced my strength along the way,
   he has cut short the days allotted to me.
24 Do not take me when only half my life remains,
   you whose years are unlimited.
25 At the beginning you laid the foundations of the earth,
   and the heavens are the work of your hands.
26 They shall perish, while you remain;
   like a garment they will wear out.
   Like clothes you will change them,
   and they will be used no more.
27 But you are the same for ever;
   your years will never end.
28 Your servants' children will continue,
   their posterity will endure for ever in your presence.

This difficult psalm seems to jump from one subject to another;
from the psalmist's physical condition (verses 3–5) to his feeling
of isolation (verses 6–7), from a plight caused by enemies plotting
against him (verse 8) to the feeling that his troubles are God's
punishment (verses 9–11), from prayers that God will rebuild
Jerusalem (verses 13–16) to confident assertions that God cares
especially for the destitute and oppressed (verses 17–20). Then,
suddenly, the psalmist returns to complain about his personal
troubles, contrasting his tenuous grasp on life with the

permanence of God and of the believing community (verses 23–8). Unfortunately, it is not always clear how some of the Hebrew tenses should be translated, or how some verses should be related, or not related, to other verses.

In spite of this apparent confusion, one theme stands out clearly, that of God's permanence over against the fleeting and temporary nature of all other things, including the universe itself. The opening verses describe the transitory and uncertain nature of human existence. Life runs its course all too quickly, especially when punctuated by illness, feelings of isolation and loneliness, inevitable breakdowns in human relationships, and the feeling that even God is an enemy.

At verse 12 the focus switches from the psalmist to God. Another token of human impermanence, ruined Jerusalem, will be rebuilt by the God whose glory fills the earth and who is the only hope of the destitute and prisoners. However, at verse 23, the psalmist returns to the theme of his troubles; yet these are the prelude to magnificent contrasts, between the psalmist who has lived only half his days and God whose years are unlimited; between a universe that will grow old and a God forever young. The final verse also brings a surprise, for it suggests that even after the universe is no more, God's people will still exist. If, through his mercy, they are his people, he will ensure that their generations continue. Their continuance will be an aspect of God's permanence.

Users of the psalm today may find it easiest to relate to the opening eleven verses and the final five. As opposed to the psalmist's lively sense of the fragile nature of his own existence and the permanence of God, modern society tries to pretend that human lives and institutions are indestructible. Vast sums of money are spent in the rich countries on treatments designed to arrest or mask the effects of the passing years. Growing weakness is something that people admit reluctantly, if at all. It is only when people accept that life is limited, characterized by weakness, and ultimately ended in death, that they can begin to live it responsibly.

Psalm 130

1 From the very depths I call to you, Lord.

2 Lord, hear my prayer.
   Let your ears be attentive
   to the voice of my plea for help.

3 If you, Lord, take note of our wrong-doings,
   who can survive?

4 But it is your nature to forgive;
   therefore are you held in awe.

5 I wait for the Lord,
   my soul waits for him
   and in his word I put my trust.

6 My soul waits for the Lord
   more than watchmen look for the morning.

7 Trust in the Lord, O Israel,
   for with the Lord is unfailing love,
   and great is his power to deliver.

8 He alone can deliver Israel
   from all their wrong-doings.

The key word in this psalm comes in verses 3a and 8b, and is translated here as 'wrong-doings'. Other versions have 'what is done amiss' (PBV), 'iniquities' (AV, NRSV), or 'sins' (NEB, NIV). The Hebrew word appears to mean actions which deserve to be punished, and the guilt that accrues from committing such actions. Depending on which sense of the word is emphasized, and both are possible, the psalmist is either experiencing some kind of physical punishment or suffering, because of having done wrong, or is weighed down by an enormous burden of guilt. In both cases the punishment or guilt may, in fact, be unconnected with specific wrong-doings. It is easy for people to feel guilty unnecessarily, or wrongly to attribute suffering or misfortune to things that they have done or failed to do.

One way of taking the psalm is to see it as the cry of Israel during the Babylonian exile, when it was widely believed that the exile was the result of the wrong-doings of the people of God over a number of previous generations. This makes excellent sense historically, but hardly connects with contemporary daily life. Our use of it is more likely to be psychological than physical, that is, we are much more likely to be weighed down by anxiety than to find ourselves being physically punished for having done wrong; and in today's world, at least, mental pain can be just as disabling as physical pain.

How can this psalm help us, then? Its opening words 'From the very depths I call' indicate that the psalmist has reached the very limits of mental or physical endurance, and that God can yet meet him where he is. If we have remotely similar feelings then we are not the first, or only, ones to have experienced them, and there is no reason why God cannot meet us there, either. Secondly, the psalm is not about forgiveness of sins in the sense of wanting God to overlook or condone genuinely wrong things that we may have thought or done. It is about God accepting us in our weakness (compare verse 3), with that acceptance becoming the strength that carries us through our troubles. The realization that God in his majesty has a concern for wounded and fragile individuals leads to awe (verse 4), one of the most important features of any relationship with God.

Psalm 143

1   Hear my prayer, Lord,
     give ear to my pleas;
     answer me in your righteousness,
2   and do not bring your servant to judgement,
     for no living person can be justified in your sight.
3   The enemy pursues me,
     he crushes my life to the ground,

he makes me dwell in darkness
like those long dead.

4   My spirit grows faint;
my heart within me is desolate.

5   I remember the days of old,
I meditate on all your works;
I consider the work of your hands.

6   I stretch out my hands to you;
my soul longs for you,
as for a thirsty land.

7   Hasten to answer me, Lord,
my spirit fails.
Do not hide your face from me,
or I shall be like those who go down to the pit.

8   Make me hear your unfailing love in the morning,
for in you I trust.
Show me the way that I should go,
for to you I lift my soul.

9   Deliver me from my enemies, Lord;
with you I seek refuge.

10 Teach me to do your will,
for you are my God.
Your spirit is good;
may it lead me along an even path.

11 For your name's sake,
preserve my life, Lord;
for your righteousness' sake
bring my soul out of trouble.

12 And in your steadfast love
slay my enemies,
and destroy all those who vex my soul;
for I am your servant.

In the present psalm it is not clear who the psalmist's enemies are. Are they actual people who physically threaten him? Are they an illness that has brought him to death's door (verse 3)? Or are the enemies thoughts and anxieties that restrict the psalmist's vision and make the future seem bleak (verse 4)? The answer is potentially 'yes' to each of these possibilities; yet what the psalmist seems to fear most of all is that he should find himself without God in the world. While it is true that he would prefer to live in a world from which his enemies are absent, so that he even asks God to destroy his enemies in language that is difficult for modern readers (verse 12), his need for God is not simply a need for a deliverer. It is not the case that as soon as, or if, God hears his prayers and delivers him from whatever is troubling him, the psalmist will get back to living a 'normal' life in which God has little or no place. The psalm is a heartfelt cry for God's presence. To be without God is like longing for water in a dry land (verse 6), like wishing that the night would soon end and the morning come with the promise of the warmth and sunshine of a new day (verse 8). The psalmist does not want to live a life from which God is excluded or in which he is marginalized. At the same time he realizes that being with God involves a structured way of life, not simply a mystical presence. Thus he prays for God to show him the way in which he should walk; he asks for God's spirit to guide him along the even path. The psalm, then, challenges modern users to ask why they want God at all. Is it merely as a last-resort solution to physical or mental difficulty, or is it because without God, life is empty as well as potentially difficult? Few of us will be able to say honestly that we feel the absence of God as keenly as we would feel the absence of a friend or loved one; in which case we need to ask ourselves searching questions about our belief in God and its aims and purpose.

4

Psalms of Zion

Psalm 46

1   God is our hope and strength,
     a help in trouble ready to be found.

2   Therefore we do not fear if the earth heaves,
     and mountains are carried into the midst of seas:

3   if their waters thunder and foam,
     and mountains quake at the swelling of the sea.

4   There is a river whose streams bring joy to the city of God,
     the Most High's holy dwelling.

5   God is in her midst, she will not be shaken;
     God will help her as sure as morning comes.

6   Nations roar and kingdoms shake;
     God utters his voice,
     the earth melts.

7   The Lord of hosts is with us;
     the God of Jacob is our refuge.

8   Come and see the works of the Lord,
     who has brought destruction on the earth.

9   He makes wars to cease to earth's ends,
     he shatters the bow and breaks the spear,
     and burns the shields with fire.

10 Cease action, and learn that I am God,
     exalted among the nations,
     exalted over the earth.

11 The Lord of hosts is with us;
     the God of Jacob is our refuge.

The key to this psalm is the refrain that occurs at verses 7 and 11, and possibly originally after verse 3. The confident assertion of God's presence gives reassurance to the psalmist when the world seems to be collapsing literally or figuratively (verses 2–3), or when the nations seem set to destroy each other in war (verse 6). The reference to the river that gladdens the city may be to the Gihon spring that supplied Jerusalem with water, and which still flows to this day. It becomes a symbol of life-giving permanence in the midst of an uncertain world. However, 'God with us' is a challenge as well as a comfort, and it certainly became a licence for complacency and even injustice at some points in Israel's history. Micah, for example, is highly critical of Jerusalem's corrupt judges, priests and prophets who 'lean upon the Lord and say, "Is not the Lord in the midst of us? No evil shall come upon us"' (Micah 3.11). This an example of a false confidence, whereas what is needed is an attitude that does not feverishly try to grasp from God what he has already promised, but one which accepts in humility, awe and wonder the truth that God wishes to be involved for good with his creatures, in spite of all their weaknesses and imperfections. We have to learn to say 'God is our hope and strength' in precisely that spirit.

For the psalm raises the question why we want a God at all. Do we want one because we hope that he will make us happier and more secure in human terms; or do we hope for a better world, whose realization may demand sacrifices from us? The psalm points towards the latter answer. It gives us a glimpse of that better world, from which wars have been banished (verses 8–9), and in which humans have ceased to believe that they alone hold in their hands the world's destinies (verse 10). Ultimately, true confidence in God's presence is a gift that comes from him. Psalm 46 may be a way of helping us to receive that gift.

Psalm 48

1   Great* and worthy to be praised
     is the city of our God;
     his holy hill
2   beautiful in its height,
     gives joy to the whole earth.
     The hill of Zion on the north side
     is the city of the Great King.
3   God in its palaces is renowned as a sure defence.
4   Indeed, the kings of the earth met together,
     and joined forces;
5   but when they saw, they were astonished;
     they were terrified and fled in alarm.
6   They were seized with trembling,
     and were in pain like a woman giving birth,
7   as when an east wind shatters ships of Tarshish.
8   What we have heard, we have also seen
     in the city of the Lord of Hosts,
     the city of our God.
     God will uphold it for ever.
9   We celebrate your unfailing love, O God,
     in the midst of your temple.
10   As your name is great, O God,
     so is your praise to the ends of the earth.
     Your right hand is full of justice.
11   The hill of Zion rejoices,
     the daughters of Judah are glad
     because of your judgements.
12   Walk about Zion and encompass her,
     count her towers,
13   take note of her ramparts,
     pass through her palaces;
     that you may tell a later generation
14   that this God

is our God for ever and ever.
He it is who will guide us for ever and a day.

* omitting 'the Lord'

Greatness is relative, just as whiteness is relative, as TV adverts used to try to convince us. If all that we have ever known as greatness is suddenly confronted with something far grander, it becomes necessary to revise all our standards. Given that most Israelites had little opportunity to go more than a few miles from their subsistence villages during their lifetimes, those that did see Jerusalem and its buildings must have been truly impressed. Yet from a modern perspective, one that benefits from travel and books on archaeology, it has to be admitted that Jerusalem was small and insignificant within its own time and world. It would have been easy for Israelites to encompass Jerusalem (verse 12); to have tried to do the same for Nineveh with its walls stretching for a number of miles would have been far more difficult!

But this type of comparison, which serves mainly to indicate how *small* Jerusalem was, raises an important question. Why was it that this comparatively insignificant settlement achieved what the mighty cities of Babylon, Assyria and Egypt were unable to achieve? Why was it able to survive destruction by sustaining a people and their religion in a way that profoundly affected the whole course of human affairs? The question can, of course, be answered without considering its religious dimension, although whether the answer will ever be convincing is another matter. If the religious dimension is allowed, however, the answer is that God was somehow involved in the affairs of Jerusalem in a way that he was not involved with Nineveh or Thebes.

If we approach the psalm in this way it may begin to make sense for today's world. Measured in terms of its own times, Jerusalem was not big, not outstandingly beautiful and certainly not the kind of place that struck fear into the hearts of its adversaries (compare verses 4–7). Measured in terms of history, however, Jerusalem was able to outlast all its foes and become a symbol of hope; and this was possible not because of the city's natural qualities but because of Israelite belief that it was the earthly link with the universal God of justice (verse 10), who had chosen and would guide his people (verse 14). The psalm, then, is not so much a psalm about a city, as a psalm about God, and about how anything with which he becomes involved will receive a value that will exceed anything that humans can bestow.

Psalm 76

1   In Judah God is renowned,
    his name is great in Israel.

2   In Salem is his tabernacle,
    and in Zion his dwelling-place.

3   There he broke the lightning arrows of the bow,
    the shield, the sword and battle itself.

4   You are awesome and mighty,
    coming from the hills of prey.

5   The mighty ones are plundered;
    they sleep their sleep,
    and the valiant ones have not found their strength.

6   At your rebuke, O God of Jacob,
    both horse and rider sleep death's sleep.

7   You are awesome;
    who can stand before you when you are angry?

8   You make your sentence heard from heaven;
    the earth fears and is silent,

9   when God arises for judgement
    to deliver all the poor of the earth.

10 The wrath of man shall praise you;
    you gird on the remnant of anger.

11 Make vows to the Lord your God and keep them;
    let those around him bring gifts to the awesome one.

12 He curtails the anger of princes,
    and is awesome to the kings of the earth.

Among the difficulties found in the psalm is the question whether verse 10 refers to God's wrath and anger or whether there are references to the kingdoms of Edom in southern Judah and Hamath in Syria; for it is possible to render verse 10 as 'the wrath of Edom will praise you, the remnant of Hamath will celebrate (or, with the remnant of Hamath shall you gird yourself)'. If there are references to Edom and Hamath, then the psalm either records an unlikely Israelite victory over enemies at two geographical extremes (far south and far north) or Edom and Hamath are poetic or metaphorical ways of speaking of the totality of Israel's enemies.

Whether or not specific Israelite wars are behind the psalm (commentators have suggested many possibilities) the use of military images to describe God's power and majesty is inescapable and this will be problematic for some readers, at least. Yet people today regularly view films and videos which contain considerable violence that is acceptable so long as the forces of good triumph at the end over the forces of evil.

A closer look at the psalm suggests that God's use of force in it has an essentially restraining function. He brings war to an end (verse 3) and renders the powerful powerless (verse 5). If he initiates action it is to mete out justice and deliver the poor (verse 9). The enigmatic verse 10 can be taken to mean that God can change human hostility into something more positive. The psalm, then, does not glorify war, but longs for its abolition; and it looks for the abolition to God, who is awesome and held in awe. A first step towards the abolition of war would be an acknowledgement of the claims that God legitimately makes upon us (compare verse 11). It is the lack of a transcendent perspective that encourages humans to think that they alone can control the world and other people: by force, if necessary.

Psalm 84

1   How loveable the place is where you dwell
    O Lord of Hosts!

2   My soul exhausts itself in longing
    for the courts of the Lord;
    my heart and body cry out joyfully to the living God.

3   Even the sparrow has found a home,
    and the swallow has a nest
    where she can lay her young,
    near your altars, O Lord of hosts,
    my king and my God.

4   How blest are those who dwell in your house;
    they are always praising you.

5   How blest are those who find their strength in you,
    who plan to go on pilgrimage.

6   If they pass through a cheerless valley
    it becomes a spring of water,
    and the autumn rain clothes it with blessings.

7   They go on growing in strength
    until they appear before God in Zion.

8   O Lord, God of hosts, hear my prayer;
    hearken, O God of Jacob.

9   O God, our defender, look upon us,
    and behold the face of your anointed one.

10 One day in your courts is better than a thousand elsewhere.
    I would rather stand at the very edge of the house of God
    than dwell in the tents of the wicked.

11 For the Lord God is a sun and a shield.
    The Lord gives grace and glory,
    and will not hold back what is good
    from those who live lives of integrity.

12 O Lord of hosts,
    how blest is the man
    who puts his trust in you.

This is sometimes described as a pilgrimage psalm used by pilgrims on their long journey to Jerusalem, encouraging each other en route, swelling in numbers until they finally reach the city and its temple, the goal of their aspirations (verses 5–7). This may be right; but the psalmist may also be recalling pilgrim throngs that he has seen and may be using these remembered scenes to express his own desire and longing to be in the temple which, for him, is a refuge from living among the wicked (verse 10b) and the special dwelling-place of God.

To understand some of the psalm's details we have to remember that temples in the ancient world were sets of courtyards (compare verse 2b), one or more of which contained an open-air altar or altars (compare verse 3), the only roofed building being the sanctuary, from which ordinary worshippers were usually excluded. Temples were also built, where possible, on the top of hills, so that they had to be approached by ascending sets of staircases. In this way they conveyed a sense of awesome transcendence. Inside the courtyard, however, their reality may have been closer to the noise and distraction of modern cathedrals filled with groups of tourists, than to the ideal implied in this psalm. It was once, perhaps unkindly, but not entirely inaccurately, written of the Jerusalem temple that it must have resembled a cross between a market and a slaughterhouse. One of the remarkable things about the psalms that seem to be connected with the temple is that they rarely mention the ritual slaughtering and burning of sacrificial animals that must have been so prominent a part of its daily routine. The temple, in the psalms, is a place of prayer and praise, and of delight in a God who gives hope to those who trust him. For this reason it is not out of order to read the psalm, not as a record of an ancient pilgrimage, but as an expression of the hope of arriving, at the end, in the eternal city of God.

But there is a practical challenge. It may be better to spend one day standing at the very edge of the outermost courtyard of the temple than many days elsewhere, and certainly better than living among the tents of the wicked. But for many people, life has to be lived among these tents, and for today's world the 'tents of wickedness' will include those structural features of modern life that promote greed, corruption and gross unfairness. No doubt the psalmist's vision and hopes were part of the way in which he attempted to lead a life of integrity (verse 11d) while resident among the tents of wickedness and while finding that he was passing through a cheerless valley.

Psalm 87

1   He has founded Jerusalem upon a holy hill.
The Lord loves the gates of Zion
more than all the dwelling-places of Jacob.

2   Glorious things are spoken of you,
you city of God.

3   People from Egypt and Babylon
will I include among those who know me;
indeed, people from Philistia, Tyre and Ethiopia
were born in Zion.

4   But of Zion it will be said:
each one was born there;
the Most High established her.

5   When the Lord writes down the list of the nations,
he will record 'this one was born there'.

6   They will respond in dance and song:
'To you, O God, we owe our origins'.

Psalm 87 has been described as the most difficult psalm in the Psalter to translate and interpret. In particular, verse 6 is very obscure, while it is not clear whether God or the psalmist is the speaker in verse 4. In spite of these and other difficulties, a vision of an ideal Jerusalem emerges from the psalm, an ideal Jerusalem that embraces foreign nations, and which is a

description of the kingdom of God. Against what is often regarded as the Jewish nationalism or particularism of the Old Testament, the psalm boldly declares that citizens of countries such
as Egypt, Babylon, Philistia, Tyre and Ethiopia will be regarded
as citizens of Jerusalem when God writes down the list of nations.
The image probably draws upon the practice of keeping a record
of the free citizens of a city state in the ancient world. The citizens
of Jerusalem certainly get separate mention (verse 4 – one of the
many difficulties is how to understand what the Hebrew implies
here), but this is because they are fortunate enough to have been
born in that city whose values will be coveted by all peoples of
good will.

This is a very different Jerusalem from Isaiah's whore and
house of murderers (Isaiah 1.21) or Micah's Zion built on
bloodshed (Micah 3.10); it is different from the Jerusalem implied
in Psalms 55 and 94. It is not a human creation, which is why
its citizens are not confined to those born there. In other words,
this is a psalm about grace; about something fashioned by God's
unconditional love, something that transcends the kinds of
human behaviour that led Isaiah and Micah to describe the Jerusalem they knew in such sombre terms. No wonder that those
who discover that they are citizens of this ideal Jerusalem dance
and sing (verse 6). But was the psalmist familiar with the real as
opposed to the ideal Jerusalem? Did he, or those with whom he
lived, regard Egyptians and Philistines as fellow-citizens, or did
he regard them as foreigners and potential enemies? Such is the
usual realism of the psalms that we can assume that he was familiar with the real world; and that his vision was not simply a
future hope, but also something that challenged his daily life.

Psalm 122

1   I was glad when they said to me
    we shall go to the Lord's house.
2   Our feet are standing

within your gates, Jerusalem –

3 Jerusalem that is built
as a city that is united in itself,

4 to which the tribes go up,
the tribes of Yah,
as decreed to Israel,
to praise the name of the Lord.

5 For there are set thrones for judgement,
thrones for the house of David.

6 Pray thus for the peace of Jerusalem:
'May those who love you prosper.

7 May there be peace within your walls,
serenity within your palaces.'

8 For my brothers' and companions' sake
I will pray for peace within you;

9 for the sake of the house of the Lord our God
I shall seek your good.

This psalm is organized around the twin themes of peace and unity. Jerusalem, a name associated with peace, inspires unity in the way it is built, as a gathering point for the tribes, and as a place where justice is administered. The difficult Hebrew of verse 3 is well rendered by phrases ranging from the poetic 'Jerusalem is built as a city that is at unity in itself' (PBV) to the more prosaic, but accurate, 'Jerusalem, which is built as a city, whose houses stand close together within her walls' (The Revised Psalter). Small, compact, Jerusalem is the point around which the worshippers of the God of Israel unite, and where the supreme seat of justice is located (verse 5). Peace, however, does not primarily reside in buildings, or sacred places, or institutions such as the administration of justice. Peace is an attitude of mind mediated through structures of reconciliation and mutual respect. This is why the prayer for Jerusalem's peace is centred upon the people who care for the city, and who live there (verses 6–7). Verse 9 also makes it clear that peace does not come automatically or without human effort. Even the activity of praying for peace indicates this.

Modern users of the psalm will be only too aware that Jerusalem has more often been the cause of division than unity, as religious groups have sought to gain or retain sovereignty over the city. The psalm can be read as a reminder that particular places are not ends in themselves but means. This was seen particularly clearly by prophets, who described Jerusalem not as a city of peace and justice but as the refuge of murderers (Isaiah 1.21). To pray, then, for the peace of Jerusalem is not to pray for an abstract entity or even a place that people can visit today. It is to pray that human beings will treat each other with mutual respect and recognition of justice. In this sense, the psalm has implications far beyond the peace of Jerusalem.

5

Psalms of Ascents

Psalm 120

1   In my distress I cried to the Lord,
    and he answered me.
2   Lord, deliver me from lying lips,
    from a deceitful tongue.
3   What will be done to you,
    deceitful tongue,
    and what more will you suffer,
4   you who are like the sharp arrows of a warrior,
    with tips hardened by fire?
5   Alas that I dwell in Meshech
    and inhabit the tents of Kedar.
6   Too long has my soul dwelt
    with those who hate peace.
7   I am for peace,
    but when I propose it,
    they are for war.

Until verse 5 is reached, this is a straightforward psalm. We all
know that the children's saying 'Sticks and stones may break my
bones, but names will never hurt me' is quite untrue; that we
can be deeply wounded by what people say, and that these
wounds may take far longer to heal than wounds inflicted by
sticks or stones. Often, the things that children say to each other
cruelly exaggerate truths, especially truths about the appearance
of children who may be taller, shorter or fatter than average.
Adults tend towards untruths, and tend more to say things

behind people's backs. It is difficult to defend oneself against half-truths spoken in supposed confidence. Indeed, such falsehoods can take on lives of their own, and survive their public refutation. The frustration of the psalmist can therefore readily be understood, leading to his outburst against the slanderous tongue. The language of verse 3 probably incorporates words used in an oath, and it expresses the wish that the pain being caused to the psalmist may rebound on to the head of his slanderers. This is a perfectly natural reaction; and in a moral universe it is to be hoped that the originators of slander will not for ever be unscathed by these cruel activities.

Verse 5 is a stumbling-block. Scholars identify Meshech with a people or country near the Black Sea (compare Genesis 10.2) while the people referred to as Kedar is located in the Syro-Arabian desert (Genesis 25.13). Because these locations are so far apart, it is difficult to suppose that the psalmist inhabited both of them simultaneously, or even in succession. They are therefore taken to be place names symbolic of exile in general. The psalmist is separated from his people and homeland. As if this were not bad enough, his neighbours slander him and mistake his attempts at reconciliation for weakness (compare verse 7). This no doubt gives rise to further slanders. Reconciliation is never easy and certainly not cheap; and it is easy to see how the psalmist has become weary of his present situation (verse 6).

In the arrangement of the Psalter Psalm 120 stands at the head of a set of psalms entitled 'Songs of Ascents' some, at least, of which contain references to pilgrimages to Jerusalem (compare Psalm 122). Whatever the original circumstances of Psalm 120's composition, it stands fittingly in its present position. If the name Jerusalem suggests 'city of peace', pilgrimage to it would be welcome for one who sought peace, but only dwelt among hatred (verses 6–7). A pilgrimage would help him to enjoy temporary freedom from hatred and slander, and bring him some peace and enjoyment. However, it is not possible to be permanently on pilgrimage; pilgrims have to return home, even if home is a real or symbolic exile. Getting away from life's problems for a brief spell can do wonders; but ultimately, life has to be lived where people find themselves, where their only support may come from their trust in God (verse 1).

Psalm 124

1 'Had the Lord not been on our side'
let Israel say;

2 'had the Lord not been on our side
when men rose up against us,

3 they would quickly have swallowed us alive
when their anger was kindled against us.

4 The waters would have flowed over us;
the rivers would have passed over us,

5 the insolent waters would have submerged us.'

6 Blessed be the Lord who has not delivered us up
to be a prey to their teeth.

7 We have escaped with our lives
like a bird from the fowler's snare.
The snare is broken
and we have indeed gone free.

8 Our help is in the name of the Lord,
who made heaven and earth.

The simplest way to understand this psalm is in connection with the Babylonian exile of 587–540 BCE. By rights, the tiny kingdom of Judah should not have survived the destruction of its capital city Jerusalem and the temple, together with the deportation of the king and the ruling classes. There were no Geneva Conventions or bodies of international justice in the ancient world. That the tiny kingdom not only survived but gave to the world the Hebrew scriptures is one of the great achievements, if not escapes, of all time. It is in this spirit that the psalm can be read.

It is a pilgrimage psalm; it expresses wonder at the fact that pilgrimage, and to Jerusalem, is even possible given the earlier situation of a ruined city and an exiled king. Thanks are therefore given to God without whom, the psalmist is sure, no reversal of the dire situation would have been possible.

The latter part of the psalm uses two images drawn from daily life to describe the people's plight and their deliverance from it. The first is that of violent flood waters that sweep away everything in their path. The invading armies must have seemed like that. The second image is that of a bird caught in a trap. Perhaps exile seemed like that with little apparent chance of escape. Against all the odds however, the people are free.

Today's users of the psalm may feel that it is wrongly nationalistic, in the sense of giving the impression that God is always on the side of his people, right or wrong – the kind of attitude that was prevalent in Britain and Germany during the First World War. The psalm does not itself necessarily convey this view; and it certainly does not convey it when read in the whole context of the Old Testament. After all, according to the prophetic traditions, the exile was divine punishment for Israel's unfaithfulness and the restoration was an act of God's mercy. The psalm, then, can be used by any believer as a way of thanking God for any act of mercy that has brought unexpected relief. True thanksgiving does not make us think that God is our exclusive possession. True thanksgiving leads to awe and wonder at God's mercy to undeserving servants.

Psalm 126

1   When the Lord turned the tide of Zion's affairs,
    we felt that we were in a dream.
2   Our mouths were filled with laughter,
    our tongues with joyful shouts.

They said among the nations,
'The Lord has done great things for them.'
3   The Lord has indeed done great things for us;
we are truly glad.
4   Turn again our nation's affairs, Lord,
as when rivers flow in the Negev.
5   May he who sows in tears
reap with joyful shouts.
6   May he who goes out weeping,
carrying a basket of seed,
return again with shouts of joy,
bearing his sheaves of wheat.

The translation of verse 1 has been much discussed, with modern opinion not favouring the traditional rendering 'When the Lord turned again the captivity of Zion'. Nonetheless, the best way to understand verse 1 is in terms of the ending of the Babylonian exile in 540 BCE. This was such a momentous event that it must have made people at the time feel as though they were dreaming. The psalmist seems to look back to those times, imagining what it must have been like then, in the same way that people not alive at the time can try to imagine what it must have been like to experience the end of the Second World War. The psalmist also imagines what the surrounding nations must have thought (verse 2b) whether or not they really did at the time. At verse 3 the psalmist reaches his own times, looking back over this history and agreeing that the nation has much for which to be thankful.

His own preoccupation (verse 4) is with an unidentified national crisis. Commentators have made many suggestions as to what it might have been, from the struggles of the newly returned community in Jerusalem at the end of the sixth century, through to the persecutions suffered by the Jews under Antiochus IV in 168/7–164, but there can be no certainty; and in any case, there is a tendency among all peoples to think that things were better in the past than they are in the present.

The poetic images in verses 4b–6 allude to the abundant small flowers that are suddenly engendered by rain in the arid desert south, even if they have not flowered for years, and to the joy and celebration of the harvest that follows the hard toil of sowing and ploughing in the stony Palestinian soil. The point of these images is that the rain does come to the arid south, and that the harvest does result from sowing and ploughing. In the same way, the psalmist can be assured that the tide of affairs will once again turn in his favour.

6

Royal Psalms

Psalm 2

1   Why do the nations rage,
     and the peoples plot in vain?
2   The kings of the earth take their stand,
     and the rulers conspire together
     against the Lord and his anointed.
3   'Let us break their fetters,
     and cast from us their chains.'
4   He who dwells in heaven laughs;
     the Lord mocks them.
5   Then he speaks to them in his anger
     and terrifies them in his rage.
6   'I the Lord have set up my king,
     upon Zion my holy hill.'
7   'I will declare the Lord's decree:
     He has said to me "You are my son,
     today I have become your father.
8   Ask of me,
     and I will give nations as your inheritance;
     you will possess the far corners of the earth.
9   You will lead them with a rod of iron,
     you will break them in pieces like a potter's vessel." '
10   And now, kings, be wise,
     be prudent, you who are judges on earth.
11   Serve the Lord in awe;
     with trembling kiss the feet of the king

12   lest he is angry and you perish as you go.
       His wrath is quickly kindled;
       happy are all who find refuge in him.

This is a psalm whose modern understanding of it has opened up a gap between it and today's worshippers. It is generally accepted by scholars that the psalm must be understood in the terms of the coronation of kings in ancient Israel. On such an occasion, the king would receive a written decree which, on being read aloud, would publicly declare that the king had been adopted into a special relationship with God (verse 7). This 'sonship' gave the king not only special obligations for ruling his own people, but world-wide obligations to rule the nations (verses 8–11), granted belief in the universal sovereignty of God. That the nations were unwilling to accept this sovereignty is indicated by the opening words (verses 1–3). The death of a king and the accession of his successor was always an optimum time for anyone who wished to usurp the throne to do so. In the psalm the nations are represented as wanting to overthrow, and free themselves from, the rule of the king in Zion. The psalm asserts that this will never be possible, and that the only reasonable course open to the nations is to serve God and his king (verse 11). To some modern users of the psalm, the idea of kingship may be at best old-fashioned and at worst a symbol of male authoritarianism; and what has an ancient coronation ceremony to do with today's world? It may, in fact, be impossible to 'redeem' the psalm. It should be noted, however, that it cannot be taken literally and that even its 'plain sense' contains deliberate idealization. It was never the case that an Israelite king ruled the nations of the world, while the verdict of the Old Testament on many of the Israelite kings was that they were unfaithful to God; that is to say, whatever may have happened at their coronation, this did not guarantee that they would uphold justice, defend the poor or even seek to be faithful to God.

What is being described, then, is an ideal king exercising an ideal rule; a rule that will require the disciplining of the nations to the extent that they are corrupt and unjust; a rule that will to that extent be resented and opposed by the nations. This brings us to a situation not too far removed from today's world, a world where danger comes to the planet and its inhabitants not only from some nations, but from the powerful economic interests embodied in multi-national companies that seem to be responsible for no one, and which regard human beings as disposable means in the pursuit of global power. It may be possible to use the psalm, then, as a prayer for a just universal order, based upon the inalienable dignity of human beings. For the God who says to the king 'You are my son', says to all members of the human race, 'You are my daughters and my sons.'

Psalm 20

1 May the Lord answer you in the time of trouble;
   may the name of the God of Jacob exalt you on high.

2 May he send you help from the sanctuary,
   and support you from Zion.

3 May he remember all your offerings,
   and find your burnt offerings acceptable.

4 May he give you your heart's desire,
   and bring all your plans to fruition.

5 May we rejoice in your salvation,
   and set up our banner in the name of our God.
   May the Lord grant all your requests.

6 Now I know that the Lord delivers his anointed.
   He answers him from his holy heaven
   with the saving strength of his right hand.

7 Some opt for chariots, others for horses,
   but we rely on the name of the Lord our God.

8 The others bow and fall down,
   but we stand up and gain strength.

9   Save the king, Lord;
     answer us when we call to you.

This psalm is not as straightforward as it seems. On the face of it,
it is a prayer spoken on the eve of battle. A congregation addresses the king, expressing their hope that he will have God's
support. Reassured by a prophetic word, the king declares his
confidence that prayers have been heard (verse 6) and that victory
is consequently assured. The congregation declares trust in God
to be superior to reliance on military hardware (verse 7), and the
psalm ends with a renewed prayer on behalf of the king.

The problem with this interpretation, convincing as it is, is to
know how, and indeed whether, it fitted into real life. The Old
Testament has two strands of material about Israel's wars: a realis-
tic one and an idealistic one. The former recognizes that the Israelites lose battles; indeed, the prophets often envisage defeat as a
divine punishment for Israel's disobedience (e.g. Amos 4.2–3;
5.1–3; 6.11–14; Jeremiah 25.8–14). The idealistic strand is found
in books such as Joshua, Judges and Chronicles, where the role
of the Israelite armies is minimal, and the victory is achieved by
God, provided that the people are faithful. Psalm 20 seems to fit
better with the idealist strand. If it really was used on the eve of
actual battles, it was a communal ritual, whose social function
was to bring reassurance to the combatants. Defeat must have
raised doubts about its efficacy.

If the psalm belongs to the idealistic strand, how can it help today's users? It links the psalm with the perennial story about the
struggle of good and evil, which is the dominant feature of
modern films and novels, and which expresses a deep human longing for a better world. These types of story-telling, important in
any age, fulfil a deep need, yet leave a credibility gap. For
although battles against evil are always won, the war is never
ended; and the use of violence to overcome evil is never conclu-
sive. To rely on God rather than horses and chariots may not
make much sense as military tactics, but it does make sense if
one believes that only God can ultimately redeem the world.

Psalm 45

1 My heart bubbles over with fine words.
As I recount the deeds of the king
my tongue is the pen of the skilled scribe.

2 You are more handsome than any other man;
grace flows from your lips,
therefore God has blessed you for ever.

3 Gird your sword upon your thigh, mighty warrior,
in honour and splendour,

4 and may your splendour bring you success.
Ride on in the cause of truth
and for the sake of justice,
and may your right hand teach you awesome things.

5 Your arrows are sharp and pierce the hearts of the king's
enemies;
people fall beneath you.

6 Your throne is established like God's throne,
for ever and ever.
The sceptre of your kingdom
is a sceptre of justice.

7 You love what is right and hate what is evil.
Therefore your God has anointed you
with the oil of gladness above your companions.

8 Your garments are fragrant with myrrh, aloes and cassia.
Music from palaces inlaid with ivory makes you glad.

9 The daughters of kings form your entourage,
the queen mother at your right hand wears finest gold.

10 Hear, O daughter; consider and give ear.
Forget your own people and your father's house.

11 The king will desire your beauty,
for he is your lord and you must honour him.

12 The cities of Tyre and the richest of the people
will seek your favour.

13 Within the palace the king's daughter is gloriously apparelled,
      her clothing embroidered with gold.

14 Wearing richly coloured robes she is brought to the king,
      her virgin companions in her train are brought to you.

15 They are brought with joy and gladness
      and enter the king's palace.

16 Instead of your fathers you will have sons,
      and make them princes over the whole earth.

17 I will make your name known to every generation;
      therefore peoples will praise you for ever and ever.

This psalm is unambiguously about a royal wedding and may, therefore, have been used regularly on such occasions. The speaker may have been an official at the ceremony, or a professional singer who provided in song the equivalent of a modern commentary on the events. Verses 2–9 are addressed to the king in extravagant language. Whether or not he really was the most handsome man in the land (verse 2) this was how poetic convention demanded that he be described. Again, whether he had been the most just king, or the most successful in battle (verses 4b–5) was beside the point. A royal wedding, like a coronation, blurred reality in the direction of idealized language and heightened hopes.

Verses 10–12 are addressed to the bride, who is evidently foreign, if 'your own people' is taken literally. She is promised, in verse 12, that rich foreign cities will honour her. As against the reservations that some users of the psalm will have regarding language of submission in verse 11, it can be pointed out that, contrary to current practice, it is the male king rather than the female bride whose beauty and appearance are praised most.

In verses 13–15 we have a commentary on that part of the ceremony in which the bride, surrounded by her maiden companions, is brought into the royal palace, so that the actual marriage ceremony can take place. It is just possible that verse 16 is part of what is said by an official at the ceremony. British history of the past 500 years shows how important it was for a royal marriage to produce a male succession, and ancient Israel was no exception. Verse 17 may be spoken by the psalmist or an official to the king. It may also be spoken by the king to God, as part of his wedding vows.

Royal weddings are still newsworthy, and especially on the continent of Europe there is an abundance of popular magazines that are mainly devoted to the actual or imagined futures of members of royal families. Why should there be so much interest in these things? 'Royals' are often young and glamorous, with affluent life-styles. They inject colour and intrigue into the drabness of everyday life. They titillate us in the way that happily married men and women derive pleasure from reading 'love-line' advertisements by people seeking ideal partners. There is no harm in allowing people to whose glamour we could never aspire being for us symbols of human achievement. In the world of the Old Testament, however, it was not kings that caused God's name to be known to every generation (verse 17). Indeed, when the Psalter was finally compiled, probably in the second century BCE, there had been no king for hundreds of years, although Jewish monarchy would be revived in 104 BCE and last for a century and a half. The people whose service to their God's cause was greatest were the prophets – often the sharpest critics of kings, and they certainly lacked the magnificence described in the psalm. We are entitled, then, to indulge our fancies as we read the psalm; but we must also admit that it speaks of a hollow world, like rich food that may ultimately harm our health.

Psalm 72

1   Give the king your skill in judgement, God,
     your justice to the king's son.

2   May he judge your people fairly,
     and your poor with justice.

3   May the mountains be bearers of peace,
     and the hills produce righteousness.

4   May he fairly judge the poor among the people,
     and deliver the children of the needy,
     crushing the oppressor.

5   May he enjoy long life like the sun,
     like the moon for all generations.

6   May he be like rain coming down upon ripening crops,
     like showers watering the earth.

7   May justice flourish in his days,
     and prosperity multiply,
     till the moon is no more.

8   May he rule from sea to sea,
     from the great river to the ends of the earth.

9   May his enemies bow down before him,
     and his foes lick the dust.

10   May the kings of Tarshish and the isles bring him tribute,
     the kings of Sheba and Seba bring their gifts.

11   May all kings fall down to him in obeisance,
     may all nations serve him.

12   He will rescue the needy when they cry out,
     the poor and whoever has no helper.

13   He will look with compassion
     upon the helpless and needy,
     and will save the lives of the poor.

14   He will deliver them from oppression;
     precious in his sight is their blood.

15   May he live long,
     and be given gold from Sheba.
     May prayer be continually offered for him;
     may he be blessed every day.

16   May there be abundance of wheat in the land,
     may it ripple on the mountain tops;
     may it be as fruitful as Lebanon,

and blossom in the city like the grass of the earth.

17 May his name live for ever,
his renown spread while the sun endures,
and may all people find blessing through him,
all nations call him blessed.

[verses 18 to 20 are a doxology which concludes book II of the Psalter]

This psalm is a prayer, not so much on behalf of a king, but to God that the people might have an ideal king. Because of the time and place of its composition it is framed in terms of the geography, history and environment of the region. Sheba and Seba (verse 10) are references to South Arabia (modern-day Yemen), the great river (verse 8) is probably the Euphrates, while Tarshish and the isles (verse 10) are areas or countries in the far west, from an Israelite perspective. Again, the hopes for material prosperity are cast in terms of abundant rain at the most propitious times of the year (verse 6) and abundance of wheat, even in places where it would not normally flourish (verse 16). The desire for victory over enemies (verses 9, 11) is no more ambitious than some of the sentiments in the British national anthem. The predominant theme of the psalm, however, is that of justice. The opening words ask that the king may have God's own skill and impartiality in matters judicial (verse 1), and there is especial emphasis upon the king's not only ensuring proper justice for the poor and needy (verse 4) but taking active steps to be their defender (verses 12–14).

This, in fact, is a very modern psalm in the sense that power in today's world is still concentrated in the hands of a very few people; that decisions taken by even elected leaders can have significant consequences for millions of citizens. If the content of the psalm is compared with the promises made by those seeking election to high office it is likely that their manifestos will give less prominence to fairness and justice than is contained in the psalm. It would be interesting to see what sort of composition liturgists would produce who had to write a prayer for an ideal ruler in today's world. It may be legitimate to doubt whether it would be superior to Psalm 72 in either content or poetic power.

Psalm 110

1   An oracle of the Lord to my lord:
    'Sit at my right hand
    until I make your enemies
    a stool for your feet.'
2   The Lord extends the rod of your power from Zion.
    Rule in the midst of your enemies!
3   Your people offer themselves freely
    on the day of your battle.
    You are arrayed in holy garments;
    upon you is the dew of youth
    as from the womb of the morning.
4   The Lord has sworn and will not relent:
    'You are a priest for ever
    after the order of Melchizedek.'
5   The Lord at your right hand
    will shatter kings on the day of his wrath.
6   Majestically he will judge the nations;
    he will shatter heads over the wide earth.
7   He will drink from the brook on the way;
    thus will he lift up his head.

Parts of this psalm are impossible to translate and what is offered above, especially in verse 3, is guesswork. The rendering given here takes verse 3 to refer to warfare; but it is possible to translate it quite differently in terms of the king's 'birth', that is, his coronation, when he was adopted into a special relationship as

God's son. If this is what the psalm is about, verse 3 might be rendered:

> You are noble on the day of your birth,
> upon the holy mountain;
> you come from the womb of the morning,
> covered with the dew of your youth.

It is also possible to connect the reference in verse 7 about drinking from the brook with the fact that the coronation of Solomon, at any rate, is placed at the site of the Gihon stream (1 Kings 1.38–40). It is not impossible that coronation ceremonies involved the king drinking water from the stream upon which Jerusalem depended.

The best-known verse in the psalm is probably verse 4: 'You are a priest for ever, after the order of Melchizedek.' This is because of its use in the New Testament Letter to the Hebrews (Hebrews 5.6—7.28), where it enables the writer to interpret the death of Jesus in priestly terms. Within the Old Testament context the psalm has been understood to have been used to bestow upon Jerusalem kings certain priestly rights and privileges. Users of the psalm today will probably find it difficult to get much help from linking it with ancient ceremonies. A possible approach, however, is to think of the hopes that are generated in our countries when there is a change of government. Those hopes are supported by the feeling that things cannot really get worse, that the previous government had become tired and worn out, and that the promises made by the incoming ruler or rulers ought to be given a chance. The psalm contains something of this kind of hope, especially if the coronation interpretation is correct, and we concentrate upon phrases such as 'womb of the morning' and 'dew of your youth' in the alternative rendering of verse 3.

New hopes on the occasion of new beginnings are desires for a better world; that they are quickly dashed in the real world is because our trust that humans can really produce a better world is misplaced, and misplaced because spiritual resources such as trust, forgiveness, and profound respect of persons are almost totally ignored. The psalm does not help us here, with its imagery of warfare. Its reference to priesthood provides a more promising avenue, provided that priesthood is seen as something that involves all human beings in spiritual values, and something that is based on serving others, not lording it over them.

Psalm 132

1   Lord, remember for David's sake
      all his deeds.

2   How he swore to the Lord,
      and vowed to the Mighty One of Jacob:

3   'I will not enter the shelter of my house,
      nor climb upon my outspread couch;

4   I will not allow my eyes to close in sleep,
      nor my eyelids to enjoy slumber,

5   until I have found a resting-place for the Lord,
      a sanctuary for the Mighty One of Jacob.'

6   We heard of it indeed in Ephrathah,
      we found it in the fields of Jaar.

7   Let us go into his sanctuary,
      let us bow ourselves low at his footstool.

8   Rise up, Lord, into your resting-place,
      you and your mighty ark.

9   Let your priests be clothed with righteousness,
      and let your faithful servants shout aloud for joy.

10 For the sake of your servant David,
      do not reject your anointed.

11 The Lord swore an oath to David,
      in truth he will not turn from it:
      'One from the fruit of your body
      will I set upon your throne.

12 If your sons keep my covenant
      and my statutes that I teach them,
      their sons also will sit upon your throne

for evermore.'

13 For the Lord has chosen Zion,
he longs for it to be his dwelling-place.

14 'This is my place of rest for evermore;
here will I dwell,
for that is my desire.

15 Her provisions will I richly bless,
her poor will I satisfy with bread.

16 Her priests will I clothe with salvation,
and her faithful servants will truly shout for joy.

17 There will I make to sprout again the horn of David,
and prepare a lamp for my anointed.

18 His enemies will I clothe with shame,
but upon his head his crown will shine.'

The main difficulty in interpreting this psalm is to identify the 'it'
of verse 6. About what did people hear in Ephrathah? What was
found in the fields of Jaar? One answer is that 'it' was the ark of
the covenant, and that the psalm contains the liturgy for re-
enacting the story of 2 Samuel 6, the story of David bringing
the ark of the covenant to Jerusalem. On this view, there was an
annual or periodic re-enactment of the story, with the ark being
taken to Kiriath-jearim, where it was 'found' and brought
solemnly to Jerusalem. Some commentators regard Psalm 24 as
the liturgy that was used when the ark and its bearers reached
the gates of Jerusalem. The ark was then placed in the sanctuary
to the accompaniment of the words 'Rise up, Lord, into your resting-place, you and your mighty ark' (verse 8).

There are two problems with this attractive interpretation. The
first is that the Hebrew suffix for 'it' in verse 6 is feminine whereas
the word for ark is masculine (although there are two instances
where it is apparently feminine). The more serious difficulty is
that the psalm reads as though it was composed when there was
no Davidic king, and possibly no functioning temple. Verse 17,
if it is not a later expansion, certainly implies that the line of
David is broken and needs to be made to sprout once more.

The word 'there' in verse 17 even hints at the psalm originating from somewhere other than Jerusalem, perhaps a place of exile. But the difficulty does not rest on verse 17 alone. The whole tenor of verses 11–16 is that God has promised that there will be a Davidic line if it is faithful to his covenant, and that God's great desire is to have his dwelling-place in Jerusalem. Such sentiments only make sense if these conditions do not obtain. Moreover, the opening verses, asking for God's favour because of what David once did, support the idea that the psalm is a prayer for the restoration of his dynasty. In this case, verses 6–8 may derive from a ceremony that once re-enacted the bringing of the ark to Jerusalem, but they cannot determine the whole interpretation of the psalm.

If it is correct to see the psalm as a composition from exile expressing hope for the restoration of David's line and the rebuilding of Jerusalem, the closest parallel in today's world will be with people who have no independence and who long for national sovereignty. Within Britain, the impulses that have led to the setting up of a Scottish Parliament and a Welsh Assembly can also be cited, as can nationalist movements in former Yugoslavia and other parts of Europe and the Middle East. People in exile understandably feel that a foreign power cares for them less than would government by their own people. Whether or not this is true, of course, is arguable. Leaders of nationalist movements are as prone as any other leaders to be corrupted by power, and to use nationalist sentiments to further their own ambitions. This problem is not only well known to the Old Testament, but expressed in this psalm. The conditional promise, that there will be a Davidic line if his sons are faithful to the covenant and statutes (verse 12), is an important caveat. Power is too important, and can adversely affect too many people, for it to be taken lightly; and nationalism is a bad thing if it divides the human race. God's purpose in choosing Jerusalem and the house of David is not simply to benefit one nation, but to be a blessing to the whole human race. That is the real point of praying for the restoration of David's house.

7

Other Psalms

Psalm 68

1   God arises, his enemies are scattered,
    those who hate him flee before him.

2   As smoke is dispersed when blown by the wind,
    as wax melts in the presence of fire,
    so will the wicked perish in the presence of God.

3   But the righteous will be glad and exult;
    in God's presence they will truly rejoice in gladness.

4   Sing to God, sing praises to his name;
    exalt him who rides through the deserts;
    bless his name Yah and exult before him.

5   He is father of the fatherless,
    faithful judge of widows,
        even God in his holy dwelling.

6   God provides a home for the homeless;
    he releases prisoners into prosperity,
    while those who rebel against him remain in desert lands.

7   O God, when you went out ahead of your people,
    when you marched through the wasteland

8   the earth shook;
    the very heavens dripped water.
    Sinai trembled before God's presence,
    the presence of the God of Israel.

9   Of your bounty, God, you showered rain;
    you prepared a land for your possession, a land exhausted.

10 Your special people settled there;
    you prepared it, God, out of your goodness, for the poor.

11   The Lord gives a word;
       the women bearing tidings are a great host:
12   'Kings and armies are fleeing, yes, fleeing;
       the woman at home divides the spoil,
13   and cursed are you if you stay by the sheepfolds.
       There are images of doves with silver-covered wings,
       their pinions overlaid with yellow gold.'
14   When the Almighty put kings to flight,
       it was like snow falling on Mount Zalmon.
15   The mountain of Bashan is a mountain of God,
       a mountain of peaks is Bashan.
16   Why do you envy, O mountain of peaks,
       the mount God has chosen to dwell;
       the place where the Lord will for ever abide?
17   The chariots of God are ten thousand twice,
       and thousands doubled and more;
       with them came the Lord from Sinai,
       to his holy place.
18   You went up on high,
       led captive your enemies
       and received tribute from men;
       but rebels will not dwell in the presence of God.
19   Blessed be the Lord who daily bears our burdens,
       even the God who delivers us.
20   God is for us a God of salvation,
       the Lord, our escape from death.
21   He will smite indeed the heads of his enemies,
       the hairy scalps of those who walk in wickedness.
22   The Lord said 'I will bring back from Bashan the wicked,
       bring them back from the depths of the sea,
23   that you may dip your feet in their blood,
       the tongues of your dogs in the blood of your enemies.'
24   Your processions are seen, O God;
       your processions in the sanctuary,
       my God and my King.

25 The singers go first with musicians at the back;
   in the midst are the maidens with the timbrels.
26 In the congregations they bless God,
   the Lord who is Israel's fount.
27 The small tribe of Benjamin leads,
   the princes of Judah wear festal clothes,
   likewise the princes of Zebulun and Naphtali.
28 Give the command, O God,
   display your might,
   you who have done great things for us.
29 Command from your temple in Jerusalem;
   kings will bring tribute to you.
30 Rebuke the beast of the reeds,
   the company of wolves, the rulers of peoples;
   tread down those greedy for money,
   scatter peoples that relish wars.
31 They will bring tribute of bronze from Egypt;
   Ethiopia will stretch out its hands in supplication to God.
32 Sing to God, you kingdoms of the earth,
   sing praises to the Lord,
33 to the one who rides on the eternal heavens,
   and utters his voice, a mighty voice.
34 Ascribe power to God;
   his majesty is over Israel
   and his might is in the clouds.
35 Awesome is God in his sanctuary;
   the God of Israel is he,
   who gives might and strength to his people.
36 Blessed be God!

Probably no psalm contains as many problems of interpretation
yet at the same time so many memorable verses as Psalm 68.
Who cannot fail to be moved, or at least impressed, by phrases
such as 'father of the fatherless, faithful judge of widows ...
God provides a home for the homeless; he releases prisoners
into prosperity' (verses 5–6) or 'Blessed be the Lord who daily

bears our burdens, even the God who delivers us' (verse 19)? When it is asked what the psalm is actually about, there are so many different answers that it is obvious that we are in the realms of speculation. Early Christian interpreters connected the psalm with the resurrection and ascension of Christ because of the use of verse 17 in Ephesians 4.8, and understood the opening words 'God arises . . .' as a prophetic evocation of the resurrection. Jewish and later Christian interpretation sought to link the psalm to a celebration of a victory over the enemies of the people of God. The medieval Jewish interpreter Qimhi, for example, referred the psalm to the retreat of Sennacherib from besieging Jerusalem (in 701 BCE), when the angel of the Lord smote 185,000 Assyrian soldiers (2 Kings 19.35). Scholars who have used the psalms to reconstruct rituals in the Jerusalem temple have fastened upon verses such as 24–7, which speak of a joyful procession in the temple, and have associated the psalm with annual or periodic celebrations of God's kingship in which the ark of the covenant played a central role, denoting the warlike presence of God among his people. At another extreme it has been proposed that the psalm is, in fact, an index of the opening lines of a number of poetic compositions.

Anyone who is fortunate enough to be very familiar with the Old Testament will feel, as the psalm is being read or recited, that familiar passages are constantly being quoted from elsewhere in the Old Testament. The opening verse beginning 'God arises . . .' is almost word-for-word from Numbers 10.35, words spoken when the Israelites continued their journeys in the wilderness and lifted up the ark to go before them. (This is one reason why some scholars connect the psalm with a ceremony involving the ark of the covenant.) Verse 7 beginning 'O God, when you went out . . .' closely resembles Judges 5.4 and there are other allusions in Psalm 68 to the Song of Deborah in Judges 5. These allusions provide one way into interpreting the psalm and using it in daily life. It can be read as a résumé of Israel's history, a résumé that depended upon a profound knowledge of Old Testament traditions and which was designed to give warning and encouragement to users of the psalm (see also J. W. Rogerson and J. W. McKay, *Psalms* (Cambridge Bible Commentary on the New English Bible), Cambridge: Cambridge University Press, 1977, vol. 2, pp. 82–92).

By invoking the words used when the ark set forward in the wilderness, the psalm begins with the exodus and wilderness wanderings traditions, implying the deliverance of the Israelites from the armies of Pharaoh because of God's power. The call to 'Sing to God ...' (verse 4) alludes to the song of triumph sung by the Israelites following the exodus deliverance at Exodus 15. The words in verse 4 'bless his name Yah' (Yah is a shortened form of Yahweh) provide another link with the exodus, given the view of the Old Testament that it was immediately prior to the exodus that this special name was revealed to Moses (Exodus 3.14, compare also 15.3). Verse 6 refers to the rebellious Israelites in the wilderness, following the exodus.

Verses 7–17 picture God marching at the head of the redeemed people through the wilderness to Sinai (verse 8) and on to Jerusalem (verse 15), but the numerous allusions in these verses to Judges 5 are a reminder that, in the period of the Judges, Israel faced danger from many enemies before Jerusalem was finally chosen and established as the place for God's temple. Verse 11, 'The Lord gives a word ...' was, understandably, taken to be a reference to the incarnation of Christ by early Christian interpreters. It most likely refers to the fact that, in many of the Old Testament traditions about Israel's battles, it is God who instructs the armies when and how to fight and the victory is achieved by God rather than the human armies (compare Judges 5.20–1; 7.2–15). The difficult verse 13 probably contains an allusion to Judges 5.16, where Reuben is reproached for not joining in the battle. The non-combatant women who spread the news of victory and who stay by the sheepfolds divide a spoil that includes luxury items – objects overlaid with silver, and green (or yellow) gold. God's victories are likened in verse 14 to snow falling on Zalmon (a hill near Shechem; see Judges 9.48) and commentators have seen here allusions to God's power as exemplified in driving snow, or have compared lying snow with corpses of the slain lying on the battlefield. The language about Bashan (verses 15–16) probably contrasts Jerusalem with Mount Hermon, which dominates the view on Bashan (today's Golan heights). Hermon is an imposing sight with its snow-covered slopes; yet God has chosen the comparatively insignificant Jerusalem.

Verse 18 is quoted in Ephesians 4.8 with the alteration 'he (God) gave gifts to men'. In the New Testament the exaltation of Christ is seen as the means by which the Church received gifts (e.g. of the Holy Spirit). In Psalm 68 the sense is that God received gifts *from* defeated enemies.

With verses 19–23 the psalm moves from the past to the present. The God whose redeeming actions are recalled in the ancient stories and poems is a present reality, made known to the psalmist through the traditions and his own experience.

Verses 24–32 move to the future and envisage a future procession that includes not only the whole of Israel (Zebulon and Naphtali represent the northern tribes; the allusion is to Judges 4.10) but non-Israelite kings bringing gifts from their lands (verses 29, 31). The imagery for the procession (verses 24–5) is taken from Exodus 15.20, but it is also possible that the description is based upon processions that took place in the temple.

Paradoxically, a psalm that contains so much military imagery looks for the ending of wars (verse 30) and the defeat of all that threatens to disrupt peaceful and harmonious life (verse 29).

Verse 33–6 are a summons to all the kingdoms of the earth to acknowledge the lordship of God, who is both awe-inspiring (verses 34–6) and yet, as earlier verses have made clear, the defender of the marginalized (verses 5–6) and the object of close personal communion (verse 20).

How can the psalm be used today? It can be seen first of all as a reminder of the importance of history to the self-understanding of a community; and it has to be admitted that church-goers are on the whole woefully ignorant not only of the history contained in the Bible but of the history of Christianity. I regularly see Muslim children on their way to the mosque on a Saturday morning to spend some hours studying the Qur'an, and I compare that with what passes for the instruction of children and adults in the churches in Britain, and their almost paranoid commitment to 'simple faith' and to making Christianity as intellectually undemanding as possible.

But the psalm is not merely history, but a highly artistic arrangement of disparate materials into a magnificent poem, a poem that contains in summary the central statements of Israel's faith: the choosing of Israel and its deliverance from slavery, that God might establish a universal rule of peace and justice from Jerusalem, the earthly symbol of his universal sovereignty. This bare statement cannot compare with the poem in profundity even if modern readers may be uneasy at the amount of warlike imagery that it contains. The psalm is a reminder that prosaic language cannot be an adequate vehicle for either faith or liturgy. It challenges us to aspire to similar heights in our own prayers and worship.

Psalm 114

1   When Israel came out of Egypt,
      the house of Jacob from a people of strange language,

2   Judah became God's sanctuary,
      Israel his dominion.

3   The sea saw and fled,
      the Jordan turned back.

4   The mountains skipped about like rams,
      the small hills like young sheep.

5   Why was it, sea, that you fled,
      Jordan that you turned back?

6   Why, mountains, did you skip about like rams,
      you small hills, like young sheep?

7   Tremble, earth, at the presence of the Lord,
      at the presence of the God of Jacob,

8   who turned rock into a pool of water
       and flint-stone into a springing well.

It is not entirely clear whether this is a joyful or a sombre psalm. In verse 3 the (Red) sea and the Jordan evidently flee in terror; but skipping about like rams (verse 4) suggests, in English culture, at any rate, a joyful and carefree action. This fits uneasily with the 'tremble' of verse 7 and thus the NEB, for example, renders the word as 'dance', giving the psalm a joyful flavour. The view here is that this is primarily a sombre psalm, with the skipping of the mountains being a poetic reference to the shaking of the mountains when the law was given on Mount Sinai (Exodus 19.18). This brings the verse into line with verses 3 and 8, which allude to the crossing of the Red Sea, the crossing of the river Jordan and the divine provision of water during the wilderness wanderings.

If the psalm is sombre, its key is the injunction to the earth, which can be taken to include its inhabitants, to tremble at God's presence. The earth is not an independent, self-sufficient entity. It is God's creation; but this is known not by logical or philosophical reflection, but through sacred traditions about God's action in the world. God is not an absentee landlord or a detached watchmaker. God chose part of the earth as his sanctuary (verse 2) by establishing a people there that would witness to his actions. He gave them a law to be observed. These actions showed the powers of nature to be dependent upon God, not independent of him. To the questions 'Why did you flee?', 'Why did you turn back?', 'Why did you skip about?' no answer can be given. These were involuntary actions in the presence of God. It is on the basis of these things, done at particular places and particular times, that the whole earth is called upon to acknowledge God.

The particular circumstances that led the psalmist to use this call cannot be recovered. The call is valid in every generation, however. Human belief in the self-sufficiency of the world and in the right and ability of humanity to use its resources for their own ends has led to many disasters. The earth needs to learn to acknowledge its creator. The use of sacred traditions, as in this psalm, is a vital factor in the process.

Psalm 129

1   Often, from my youth up,
      have my enemies harassed me,
      may Israel say.
2   Often have they harassed me from my youth up;
      but they have not prevailed over me.
3   The ploughers have ploughed on my back,
      they have made their furrows long.
4   The Lord is just;
      he has snapped the cords of the wicked.
5   They are confounded and turned back,
      all who hate Zion.
6   They are like grass growing on rooftops
      which withers before it grows up;
7   with which the reaper cannot fill his hand,
      nor the binder gather a sheaf into his bosom.
8   No passer-by will say
      'May the Lord's blessing be upon you;
      we bless you in the name of the Lord.'

The easiest way into this psalm is to begin at the end. The last verse envisages two groups of people: passers-by and those from whom the passers-by withhold their blessing. The latter group is not blessed because it is evident that God's blessing has not favoured them. This could be explained by verses 6 and 7, if we take the unfavoured people to be not only *like* grass growing on a roof, but envisage that they were also people who endured such bad harvests that they had had to resort to trying to harvest even grass that grew sparsely on flat rooftops in almost non-existent soil. In turn, this image takes us back to verse 3, and to the long, ploughed furrows. If the harvesting image is continued the psalm is implying that long furrows yielded no harvest, and that the harvesters had to resort to drastic methods (harvesting rooftops) to get any yield.

This approach suggests two possible lines of interpretation. In the first, the attacks upon Israel by her enemies throughout her history are likened to attempts to get produce from the ground. Despite deep, long furrows (a vivid poetic description of sufferings, including exile) no harvest has been forthcoming. This was because it was carried out in malice and exploitation (compare Genesis 4.11–12), and was therefore bound to fail. The second approach sees the enemies not as foreigners attacking Israel, but as *internal* forces exploiting either the people through misrule, or the very land itself through greedy agricultural and economic policies (compare Isaiah 5.8–10). Read in this way, the psalm provides a correction to those compositions that rightly bewail the temporary ascendancy of wickedness and injustice in the world. To endure these things can bring pain and suffering. But viewed from a long-term perspective, it can be said that such violence has a limited life-span and that it brings no ultimate benefit. The world may not be a moral universe if we look at the injustices that surround us at this very moment, but a long-term view, aided by history, can enable things to be seen differently; and to be coped with more adequately.

Psalm 137

1   By Babylon's watercourses, there we sat;
    and how we wept when we remembered Zion!
2   On the poplars by their banks
    we hung our harps,

3   for there, those who exiled us
    demanded that we sing,
    our captors wanted mirth.
4   But how could we sing songs about the Lord
    on foreign soil?
5   If I forget you, Jerusalem,
    let my right hand wither away.
6   Let my tongue stick to the roof of my mouth
    if I do not remember you,
    if I do not raise Jerusalem
    above my highest joy.
7   Remember, Lord, against the Edomites
    the day of Jerusalem's destruction.
    Remember those who said
    'Strip it bare, strip it bare,
    right down to the foundations.'
8   O Babylon you destroyer,
    blessed is anyone who pays you back
    with the wrongs you have done to us.
9   Blessed is anyone who takes your children,
    and dashes them against the rocks.

The experience of being expelled from one's home and taken against one's will to a foreign country is something, alas, that people have experienced throughout human history. The twentieth century was no exception. Not only did the Second World War produce massive waves of exiles, first from west to east and then from east to west; the century ended with cruel and bitter expulsions in the Balkans and parts of central Africa. People expelled from their homes do not easily forget them. Elderly Germans travel to the Czech Republic and point out where they used to live. Elderly Palestinians retain vivid memories of the villages and lands that were once theirs.

Psalm 137 hints at the cruelty and suffering of such circumstances. It is easy to picture a group of Jewish exiles defiantly hanging up their instruments on the trees that grew by desert watercourses, as their overseers sneeringly taunted them to sing songs about Jerusalem, perhaps songs about its invulnerability (compare Psalm 46). Perhaps they had been singing songs of lament and had been interrupted by the arrival of the overseers. The passage beginning 'If I forget you, Jerusalem,' in verse 5 may be a solemn oath taken by the exiles. It could also be the words of a song that they sing in defiance of their captors.

Verse 7 makes a link between those who will not forget Jerusalem, and those who will not forget what was done to Jerusalem, when the Babylonians destroyed the city in 587 BCE. The second kind of remembering is always more bitter, because people like to remember things as they used to be, before they were destroyed and altered. The concluding verses have often been described as morally repulsive, and they have been placed in square brackets or even simply omitted when the psalm has been recited in public worship. Without in any way condoning what the verses say, it can be pointed out that they are perfectly understandable when we consider the actual situations of people who have been driven from their homes, and the way in which they retain bitter memories of those who victimized them. The reaction is a purely natural and human one. Unfortunately, it only stores up trouble for the future, as grievances become the fuel for revenge, revenge in some cases carried out long after the original events. The solution is not to tell people to forget the wrongs done to them. The solution is to work and pray for a better world, one free from exiles, captors, sneering taunts and memories that stoke the fires of vengeance. And in this better world, God is the only one who can guarantee justice for all peoples.